SMALL HOTELS AND RESTAURANTS
in Northern France and Belgium

Le Vigneron, Reims

SMALL HOTELS AND RESTAURANTS
in Northern France and Belgium

BY
MARC AND KIM MILLON

PHOTOGRAPHS BY
KIM MILLON

PAVILION

To Bella

BY THE SAME AUTHORS

The Wine & Food of Europe
The Wine Roads of Europe
The Taste of Britain
The Wine Roads of France
Flavours of Korea
The Wine Roads of Italy
The Wine Roads of Spain

Front cover: Auberge de la Grenouillère, Montreuil-sur-Mer
Back cover: Manoir du Brugnobois, near Licques

First published in Great Britain in 1994 by PAVILION BOOKS LIMITED, 26 Upper Ground, London SE1 9PD

Text copyright © Marc Millon 1994   Photographs copyright © Kim Millon 1994

Designed by John Youé and Alan Grant

A CIP catalogue record for this book is available from the British Library

ISBN 1 85793 148 3

Printed and bound in Great Britain by Butler and Tanner Ltd, Frome and London

2 4 6 8 10 9 7 5 3 1

This book may be ordered by post direct from the publisher. Please contact the Marketing Department. But try your bookshop first.

Eurotunnel would like to point out that the views of the publisher and authors of this book are not necessarily those of Eurotunnel.
Le Shuttle is a trademark of Eurotunnel.

CONTENTS

Introduction 7

Nord-Pas de Calais 16

Picardy 79

Champagne 104

Upper Normandy 125

Belgium 153

Index 186

Comment Form 189

The authors and publisher have tried to ensure
that all the information contained in this guide is as
up-to-date and accurate as possible; many of the
practical details such as addresses, telephone and
fax numbers, closing days, prices, etc., have been
supplied by the establishments themselves and are
correct at the time of writing (November 1993).
Readers should, however, always check with
establishments direct for the latest information to
avoid disappointment.
Although every care has been taken in the
preparation of this guide, no liability for any
consequences arising from the use of information
contained herein can be accepted by Eurotunnel,
the publisher, or the authors.

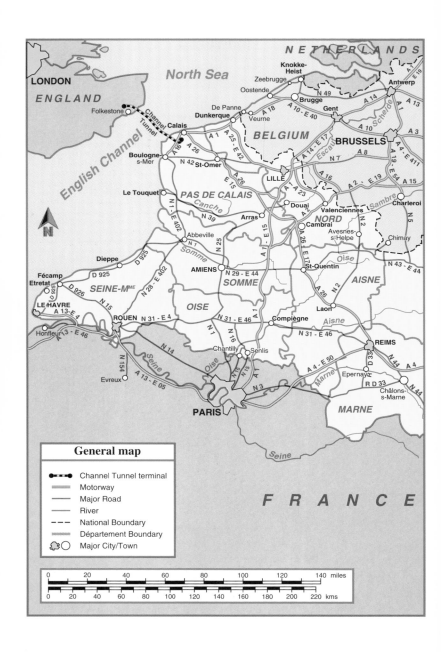

INTRODUCTION

Le Tunnel sous La Manche est arrivé !
The Channel Tunnel – the most ambitious, most expensive, most exciting private civil engineering project in history – has been completed! First dreamed about by the Academy of Amiens in 1750, later by Napoleon Bonaparte's engineers, kept alive over the centuries by courageous visionaries (some called them lunatics), today vision is reality: three tunnels each 50 kilometres long have been dug out of the bedrock of chalk-marl some 25–45 metres below the seabed connecting England with France. A complex, efficient network has been put in place for the regular and frequent operation of passenger shuttles, freight shuttles and international passenger and freight trains. Now, for the first time since the Ice Age some 12,000 years ago, Britain is physically linked to the continental European mainland.

The Channel Tunnel has aroused enormous interest among the general public. There are now over 630,000

Pas de Calais

shareholders, many of whom subscribed to Eurotunnel as founder shareholders. For those of us who did so at the time, the commitment to the Channel Tunnel was viewed as something of an act of faith: no less than a belief in its long-term importance as an integral part of a new European infrastructure which represents the future for our children and grandchildren.

The Channel Tunnel is undoubtedly one of the world's greatest civil engineering achievements. Right here on our very own doorstep to the Continent – indeed, at its busiest point of egress – it creates untold international economic opportunities certainly. Even more important than this, the Channel Tunnel tangibly improves the lives of literally millions of private individuals, those of us who cross over frequently to the Continent for pleasure, the thousands, maybe millions more, who, reluctant for whatever reason in the past, will now do so for the first and most exciting time.

Equally important as the physical link which it provides, the Channel Tunnel has also engineered something of a psychological bond between us and our continental neighbours. Europe, as we approach the next millenium, is in a state of profound, rapid and hugely exciting change. Barriers which have long stood between neighbouring states – nations which have too often found themselves at war with one another – have tumbled rapidly. Just as the dismantling of the Berlin Wall became a tangible symbol of hope for the new Europe to come, so is the completion of a fixed link between Britain and France a demonstration of supreme, technological achievement, unity, cooperation, friendship and *entente cordiale* which will carry us into the next millenium.

Le Shuttle, a Revolution in Cross-Channel Travel

On a more down-to-earth level, the Channel Tunnel represents for the traveller – especially the short-break traveller – a significant step on existing travel options. After all, the English Channel itself, *La Manche*, has been and always will remain a potent force, indeed, too often an unpredictable foe. In the nineteenth century the mere 34-kilometre journey across the Straits of Dover took up to six or seven hours. Even today, the shortest surface crossing by ferry, in sometimes windy, choppy or stormy weather, is still a miserable hour and a half too long.

Eurotunnel's Le Shuttle quite simply revolutionizes cross-Channel travel. Travel time between the two countries now takes about thirty-five minutes in the passenger vehicle shuttles. Total time from exiting the motorway in Kent to actually driving off on to a French *autoroute* or down a country lane will be reduced to just over an hour. And, of course, the very real prospect of seasickness associated with a boat crossing has been totally eliminated.

A considerable further benefit for those who prefer not to take their own vehicles is that Eurostar's new, high-speed passenger train services also pass directly through the Channel Tunnel, connecting London with Paris in about three hours and London with Brussels in over three hours. Some Eurostar trains will stop at Calais-Fréthun, connecting with lines to Boulogne and Dunkerque, while others will stop at the new purpose-built Lille-Europe station. For further information telephone the Eurostar Information Line (0233) 361 7575.

Le Shuttle Hinterland: Ideal for Short Breaks

The ease of travel, coupled with the speed and comfort of Le Shuttle and the elimination of the prospect of seasickness and physical discomfort, means that it has now become a more than feasible proposition simply to cross to Calais, Boulogne, even Brugge, for Sunday lunch, or to cross the Channel to stock up each month on French wines and Belgian beers, particularly with the advent of the EC Single Market in 1993, which gives us unprecedented shopping opportunities.

Even bearing in mind the cross-Channel fare, the fact that accommodation, food and wine are still so much cheaper across the Channel means that the total cost of a short break may still work out considerably lower than the cost of a similar holiday in the UK. Indeed, if you combine a short break with a shopping trip, the savings on wine alone could even pay for your entire

LE SHUTTLE'S TRANSPORT SERVICE

Eurotunnel's cross-Channel Le Shuttle services operate on a turn-up-and-go basis, regardless of sea conditions, twenty-four hours a day, every single day of the year, between terminals at Folkestone and Calais. Passenger vehicle shuttles carry cars, coaches and motorcycles in either single- or double-deck carriages, depending on the height of the vehicle. Separate freight shuttles carry lorries.

Once fully operational there will be up to four passenger vehicle shuttle departures per hour during peak periods. Even during the quietest periods of the night, there will always be a minimum of one departure per hour.

How to use Le Shuttle

1. Exit the M20 motorway at junction 11a straight into the Folkestone terminal. At the toll booth, purchase your ticket by cash, credit card or cheque. Tickets can also be bought in advance from travel agents or from Le Shuttle Customer Service Centre at Cheriton Parc, Folkestone, telephone (0303) 271100.

2. After passing the toll booth, you can visit the passenger terminal where you will find duty-free and bureau de change facilities as well as restaurants and shops. Alternatively, you can head directly for Le Shuttle.

3. Pass through British and French frontier controls. Both frontier controls are situated at the departure terminal only. On the other side of the Channel, you drive directly off Le Shuttle and straight on to the motorway without further frontier controls.

4. Head for the allocation area where you wait to drive on to Le Shuttle. Attendants will direct you down the loading ramp and on board. Drive through the carriages until an attendant directs you to stop.

5. Turn the engine off and put the handbrake on. Loading takes about eight minutes and then Le Shuttle departs. During the short, 35-minute journey, you remain with your car inside the spacious, well-lit, air-conditioned carriage. Stay in your car and relax, perhaps tune into Le Shuttle radio. However, you can get out of your car to stretch your legs.

6. On arrival at Calais, attendants will direct you to drive to the front of Le Shuttle and out on to the exit ramp. This leads straight to the exit road and on to the motorway network. There are no further controls and, just over sixty minutes after leaving the motorway in Kent, you are heading off into France. Remember to drive on the right!

7. On the way home, leave the A16 *autoroute* at junction 13 which leads directly to the Calais terminal. From here, you repeat the process described above.

weekend away! It is no wonder, then, that experts predict that in the next twenty years, cross-Channel traffic will more than double.

As the authors of the first Le Shuttle guides, conceived precisely to fit the needs of short-break travellers, we could not have invented a more ideal hinterland than those areas of northern France and Belgium covered in this book and its companion, *Le Shuttle Shopping for Food and Drink*. Our brief has been to cover an area fanning out in a radius of 250–300 kilometres

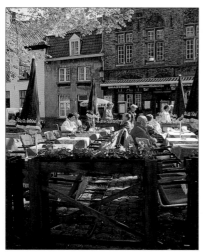

Easy come, easy go

from Calais encompassing the regions of Nord-Pas de Calais, Picardy, Upper Normandy, the wine growing part of Champagne, and much of Belgium.

Nord-Pas de Calais, the heart of both books, certainly has been a region almost wholly overlooked by British visitors in the past, rarely visited in its own right. What a delightful surprise, then, to discover that it remains wholly unspoiled, real rural France *par excellence*. From the dramatic headlands of Cap Gris Nez and Cap Blanc Nez, along the wide beaches of the Côte d'Opal; from the flat plains of Flanders, across the gentle, green, grassy hills of Artois; through the atmospheric *marais audomarois* around St-Omer to the Monts des Flandres along the Belgian frontier; and from historic inland towns and quiet fishing villages across

to the isolated and beautiful Avenois-Thiérache in the far east of the region: Nord-Pas de Calais, far from being flat, boring and industrial as it is sometimes imagined to be, is, in truth, a region with much to offer the visitor on a short break.

Picardy, the region to the south and east, is perhaps best known for its poignant battlefields which remain as silent testimonies to the two world wars. It is impossible not to be moved by the sight of so many carefully tended military cemeteries, the thought of so many young lives so tragically lost: perhaps such monuments may yet serve as something of a reminder of the follies of Man and of the continued importance of European cooperation and friendship. Once one of the great textile centres of Europe, today Picardy is a quiet, hard-working region with a host of lovely towns and cities most notable for their beautiful Gothic churches and cathedrals. Amiens, Compiègne, Laon, Noyon are indeed ideal candidates for a short, weekend break.

Champagne forms but part of the larger region of Champagne-Ardennes. We have concentrated only on the Marne *département*, especially the wine-growing areas centred on Reims, Epernay and the Vallée de la Marne. Champagne is one of the great wine regions of France and one of its most welcoming. Come here to learn about, taste and purchase Champagne at the source, to enjoy an always stylish and deliciously distinctive *haute cuisine champenoise*, and to relax in small but lovely hotels and *auberges* in wine villages or amidst the vineyards.

Visit Upper Normandy, too, and follow the tortuously winding Seine valley from the virtual outskirts of Paris, through the region's capital Rouen, up the 'alabaster coast' to Etretat, Fécamp and Dieppe. This is primarily rich, lush, agricultural country where you can live and eat well, particularly in isolated, lovely, country *auberges, fermes auberges* and *chambres d'hôtes*. Upper Normandy provides a tantalizing and delicious foretaste of the cream and cider delights of the rest of this great region extending further to the west and beyond the scope of this book.

Belgium has, in the past, been a curiously neglected tourist destination from the British point of view. Yet,

with Brussels the self-proclaimed capital of the new Europe, and with the country's proximity to the Channel Tunnel, surely this, too, is set to change. Brugge, of course, remains the most popular destination, and rightly so. This is, indeed, one of the great medieval towns of Europe, still almost wholly intact and unspoiled: how fortunate we are that it is literally on our doorstep, close enough to beckon us over again and again for a long weekend or a break of a few days. But there are many other fine cities and places to visit, too. We greatly look forward to making further discoveries in this fascinating country in future editions.

Small Hotels and Restaurants
One of the most compelling reasons for taking a short break to France or Belgium is, quite simply, to get away from it all, to go somewhere so

Rouen

Brugge canals

completely different, so utterly unlike our own everyday environment that we are able to forget all about our everyday lives. The best way we have found to achieve this is to hole up in a small, characterful hotel far from the madding crowd, somewhere that is beautiful or interesting or historic and somewhere, of course, where you can eat outstandingly well, either in the hotel itself or in nearby restaurants. These have been our basic criteria when putting this book together.

That is not to say that all of the hotels that we include are hide-away retreats, far from it. Rather, they should all, at best, have an inimitable character that is a reflection of their local area or region, as well as something of the character of the people who run the establishments. The selection is wholly and

unashamedly personal: these are the sort of places that we ourselves like to visit when we take short breaks.

We have included a broad range of types of accommodation from really beautiful, luxury hotels for a special weekend, birthday treat or anniversary, to comfortable, mainly family-run, 2-star and 3-star *Logis de France*; from conveniently located, if not otherwise particularly special, hotels which may serve primarily as overnight halts en route to somewhere else, to superior and welcoming *chambres d'hôtes*. What we have tried to find, above all, are hotels, *auberges* and *chambres d'hôtes* which, whatever their class or category, provide comfortable, clean and preferably characterful accommodation, ideally with a smile and a welcome.

As with our selection of hotels and

Auberge de la Grenouillère,
Montreuil-sur-Mer

Chambres d'hôtes

hotel-restaurants, we have sought to include a comfortable mix of restaurants catering not only for different budgets but also for different requirements and occasions. If you are like us, then there will be times when you may wish to plan a short break entirely around a really special restaurant or two. At other times, such places might be wholly unsuitable in which case we seek the simple, local, wholly typical establishment serving traditional and regional dishes in a more casual atmosphere and at more modest prices. There is no shortage of either type of establishment in the areas covered by this book and there is much in between. The principal good news is that in northern France and Belgium you can eat very well indeed, typically, authentically and in all price ranges.

One of the great finds on our travels through northern France is the number of excellent and really welcoming *fermes auberges*. A *ferme auberge* is a farmhouse restaurant almost always located in the country on a working farm where the cooking and serving is done by the farmers and their families, usually utilizing their own produce or that from neighbouring farms. It is almost always essential to reserve a table in advance; during the week, some are only open by reservation, while at weekends they are usually very crowded. The prices of the set menus are generally extremely reasonable, given the quality and the quantity of courses, and they represent excellent value. Make the effort to discover them for yourselves. We are sure you won't be disappointed.

We have also been impressed with the high standard of accommodation offered in the best *chambres d'hôtes* – the French equivalent of bed and breakfast. Many offer rooms that are individually furnished and have their own private bathrooms with bath or shower and w.c. In some cases, the *chambres* are in historic *châteaux*, in seaside town houses, in medieval city centres, even on or near wine estates. Some offer *table d'hôte* meals, home-cooked, sometimes served and eaten

LE SHUTTLE HOLIDAYS

Le Shuttle Holidays, Eurotunnel's tour-operating division, offers an attractive range of breaks, combining pre-booked accommodation with a return trip on Le Shuttle. The establishments included in this book are entirely our own personal and independent selection but, nevertheless, some of our chosen hotels can also be booked through Le Shuttle Holidays' Breaks 1994 programme. Wherever this is the case, hotels have been indicated LSHB.

For further information, and to obtain a copy of Le Shuttle Holidays' Breaks brochure, visit your local travel agent or telephone: (0303) 271717.

together with the family. An ample breakfast is always included in the price of the room. We urge you to consider *chambres d'hôtes* as an occasional alternative to hotels if they are in an area you wish to visit.

Prices

It is always difficult to give an accurate indication of prices because such information gets out of date quite quickly. On the other hand, we consider that broad price indications such as, inexpensive, moderate, expensive, are too general and imprecise to be of much real use. We have, therefore, included actual prices. You will appreciate that although they are correct at the time of writing (November 1993) they will inevitably change. Nevertheless, they give a good indication of what the prices are likely to be.

At the time of writing, the pound is approximately worth 8.50 French Francs (F) and 50 Belgium Francs (BF).

Le Shuttle Guides: A Personal Selection and a Plea for Readers' Comments

Any guide book is a reflection of the tastes, prejudices, enthusiasms and omissions of its author: this one is no exception. After all, a guide book with no personal point of view is of little more use than a phone directory. On the other hand, it is difficult – if not impossible – for anyone to be comprehensive: this book does not pretend to be an equivalent of *The Good Food Guide* or the Michelin or Gault-Millau guides (the latter two, incidentally, should be part of everyone's baggage). Alas, we have not had a team of inspectors at our disposal or an unlimited expenses budget. Many fine and in some cases well-known establishments are not included simply because we did not have a chance to visit them. We look forward to rectifying any such omission in future editions.

We have personally visited almost every establishment included in this book. Those few that we did not get to came highly recommended by locals or other reliable sources. Even so, we cannot say with our hands on our hearts that we have been able to sleep in every hotel bed or eat in every restaurant. Time and other constraints meant that this was not physically possible. Nor for that matter, can any author's judgements ever be set in stone, for one person's experiences and impressions are never quite the same as those of another.

The best and most reliable guide books, we have invariably found, are those which rely on feedback from readers, recommendations and comments made by them to keep the books current, lively and fresh. Readers' comments can fill in the gaps and can often provide personal descriptions of actual experiences which, taking the favourable with the damning, create a more valid, multi-faceted portrait of a place.

We are, therefore, actively seeking your help. At the back of this book, you will find a Comment Form and a freepost address. We would greatly

appreciate your taking the time to fill
in this form with information about
any places that you visit (both
establishments listed in this book and
new ones which you feel ought to be).
Tell us what you have liked. Tell us
what you have disliked. Tell us why.
Help us to make these Le Shuttle
guides your personal guides. (Please
photocopy the form for multiple
recommendations.)

If you find excellent food and drink
shops or farm outlets for superlative
local produce, use the same form to let
us know for the companion to this
guide, *Le Shuttle Shopping for Food and
Drink*. These two guides are intended
to be used in conjunction with each
other. Therefore, towns listed in this
volume which have entries in *Le
Shuttle Shopping for Food and Drink* are
indicated by the symbol 🛒 to make
cross-referencing easy. The numbers

preceding the town names are their
French or Belgian postal codes.

Profitons-en !
We are certain that the many fine
areas and establishments covered in
this book are places that we will all
want to visit again and again, for short
breaks, for overnight halts en route to
somewhere else, for weekend
shopping sprees, for special occasions
and celebrations, for those times when
we are just desperate to get away,
when we really need to recharge our
batteries, and for those times when we
just feel like a break for no particular
reason. The Channel Tunnel has
opened up a whole new world for us
all to discover and enjoy together.
Profitons-en !

November 1993
Topsham, Devon

NORD-PAS DE CALAIS

Nord-Pas de Calais, the region closest to Great Britain, is, paradoxically, one of the least well known regions in all of France. Many of us have, at one time or another, crossed to Calais, if only just for the day. Millions more have crossed to Calais, Boulogne or Dunkerque and, like so many lemmings, driven frantically, desperately *plein sud* without so much as a pause or a glance around. As a result, we have few definite images of the place and those we do have are usually preconceived and erroneous.

So blinkered are we that we miss countryside that is surprisingly varied, full of places which remain wholly and authentically French precisely because they have been overlooked, ignored and neglected by foreign visitors. Perhaps, for the traveller on a short break, this is its greatest asset. Because Nord-Pas de Calais remains so little known, we are able to approach it with a fresh eye, with that certain and constant sense of anticipation and discovery which always makes a trip to France, even the shortest break, so wonderfully thrilling.

Within even the shortest distances from Calais and the Channel Tunnel, there are scores of fine places and

Tulip fields near Berck-Plage

towns to visit, and no shortage either of excellent small hotels, restaurants and *fermes auberges*. Between Calais and Boulogne, the coast remains remarkably unspoiled and beautiful. Resorts and fishing villages which were popular with English visitors only decades ago but abandoned with the advent of package holidays to sunny Mediterranean destinations, today retain a rather charming, dated and old-fashioned feel about them.

Inland, even just a few kilometres from the coast, there are scores of tiny rural villages and hamlets that deserve to be discovered and explored. Between Calais and the nearby inland market town of St-Omer, there is no shortage of interesting small towns

and superbly individual hotels which make great places for a short break. Montreuil-sur-Mer located to the south of Boulogne in the lovely Vallée de la Canche, surrounded by its grassy ramparts, is rightly one of the most popular destinations for a weekend away. Sporting enthusiasts and those seeking a short activity holiday, on the other hand, may argue the case for Le Touquet and Hardelot.

Wherever you choose, a coastal or inland area, small rural village or big town or city, we are quite certain that you will receive a welcome that is genuine and warm. No other region in France, we conjecture, is set to change more quickly as the Continent realigns itself. Yet for all that, we are certain

Audresselles

that Nord-Pas de Calais, which over the centuries has seen armies and enemies come and go, surviving the ghastly onslaughts of successive wars, will retain the unspoiled charm and traditional hospitality which makes it such a friendly, easy place for visitors to enjoy. We are fortunate, indeed, that it is literally right on our own doorstep.

à Table

Nord-Pas de Calais does not immediately impress you as one of the great gastronomic regions of France. Yet this is a region where it is not at all difficult to eat especially well. For a start, there is a wealth of exceptional produce and products from both sea and land. Boulogne-sur-Mer, the premier fishing port of France, is the source of fine shellfish and fish. Inland, this region is the source of scores of other fine regional produce and products including free-range poultry from Licques; *foie gras de canard et d'oie* from Artois; excellent vegetables from the *marais audomarois* around St-Omer; smoked garlic from Arleux; scores of fine farmhouse cheeses, including such pungent classics as Maroilles, Vieux Lille, Sire de Créquy and Dauphin; regional beverages like dark, strong *bières de garde* and pungent, flavoursome genièvres; and many regional and local specialities such as *andouillettes* made with *fraise de veau* from Cambrai and

Arras; *escaveche*, a marinated fish concoction the recipe for which dates back to the Spanish occupation in the sixteenth century; cheese and vegetable tarts, breads and pastries from wood-fired ovens; and so much more.

While today, in coastal restaurants and country hotels alike, the cuisine most usually encountered is solid, traditional, *bourgeoise*, there is, nonetheless, a distinctive, regional flavour which reflects the Flemish traditions of the region. Both beef and chicken are cooked in beer, not wine (*carbonnade à la flamande* and *coq à la bière*). There are scores of typically regional dishes including *anguilles au vert* (eels cooked in parsley and other herbs), *waterzooï* (a soupy stew made with either chicken or fish) and *potjevleesch*, a tasty terrine made with pork, rabbit, chicken and veal. *Le hochepot* is the Flemish version of *pot-au-feu*, a one-pot meal containing beef, mutton, veal, perhaps a pig's foot to give it a thick, gooey texture, and lots of winter root vegetables.

In addition to traditional and regional cuisine, there are some very fine restaurants in the region where modern, innovative and inventive cuisine takes pride of place; indeed, some of these restaurants are also stylish hotels and, thus, offer the opportunity for really special, luxury breaks with superlative and exciting cuisine.

LE MENU DU TERROIR

soupe de poissons
flamiche aux poireaux
tarte au Maroilles
foie gras de l'Artois

plateaux des fruits de mer
sole meunière
caudière
la gainée boulonnaise
anguilles au vert

potjevleesch
poulet or volaille de Licques à la bière
carbonnade à la flamande
andouillette de Cambrai

Maroilles
Dauphin
Boulette d'Avesnes
La Trappe de Belval
Monts des Cats
Vieux Lille
Mimolette

tarte au gros bord
gaufres

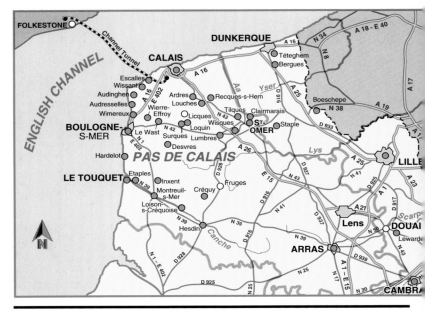

62610 ARDRES (PAS DE CALAIS)

Calais 17 km – Boulogne-sur-Mer 35 km – St-Omer 26 km

HOTEL-RESTAURANT

**Grand Hôtel-
Restaurant Clément**
91, esplanade
Maréchal Leclerc
BP 2
tel.: 21 82 25 25
fax: 21 82 98 92

The Grand Hôtel-Restaurant Clément is an *ancien relais de poste* located just off Ardres' main square and has been attracting English guests for literally decades. Today, young François Coolen and his wife Isabelle (the fourth generation to run the place) have brought new style to the Clément. While maintaining the traditional, family-style hotel, they have taken the restaurant up several notches and have in the process earned considerable acclaim both locally and nationally. François is a talented and ambitious chef, one of a select group of *jeunes restaurateurs d'Europe*. At the Clément, he serves creative, modern cuisine utilizing, above all, the fine produce and products of the Pas de Calais including superlative shellfish and fish from Boulogne, farmhouse poultry from nearby Licques, *foie gras d'Artois* and fresh vegetables from the *audomarois*.

There are sixteen bedrooms, furnished and decorated simply but traditionally, impeccably clean and rather

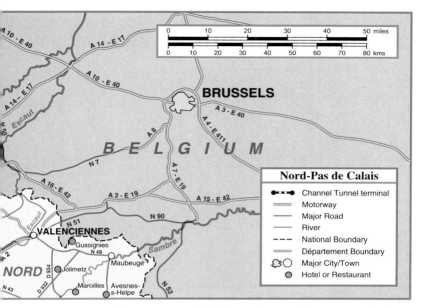

charming in an old-fashioned way. All have private bath or shower, w.c., television, telephone and mini-bar. The quieter rooms overlook the garden at the back and there is ample private parking.

Closed Mon. and 15 Jan.–15 Feb. ❖ Credit cards: Visa/CB, Eurocard/Access, American Express, Diners ❖ Rooms: double 230–330 F, breakfast 35 F ❖ Menus: 80–320 F, menu enfant 50 F ❖ à la carte: about 250 F ❖ Parking ❖ English spoken ❖ L S H B

HOTEL-RESTAURANT

Hôtel-Restaurant Le Relais

tel.: 21 35 42 00
fax: 21 85 39 36

This small, family-run hotel-restaurant located on Ardres' central, grassy square is a genuinely friendly and pleasant establishment: very simple, very traditional, very French. The good, unpretentious restaurant in the long, beamed dining room serves filling, unfussy *cuisine bourgeoise*. The 118 F menu, for example, offers *salade de gésiers confits*, *coq au vin* or *confit de canard aux haricots rouges et cèpes*, cheese and dessert. The thirteen bedrooms are clean, basic and functional, small but with their own shower cubicle and w.c., television and telephone. There are a few larger rooms

Le Relais, Ardres

with baths, too, as well as two adjoining rooms which make a family suite.

The Relais is an inexpensive stopover and a good place for simple, satisfying meals.

Open all year ❖ Credit cards: Visa/CB, Eurocard/Access ❖ Rooms: double 190–240 F, breakfast 20 F ❖ Menus: 63 F, 118 F, 175 F ❖ à la carte: about 150 F ❖ Parking ❖ English spoken

---

FERME AUBERGE

3 km S.E. at Louches

La Ferme Auberge Manoir du Rouge Camp
635, Grande Rue
tel.: 21 36 96 96

This *ferme auberge* is a good place to remember when you are hungry. It is conveniently located just off the road to Calais. While not a refined restaurant in any sense, its dishes are all made from quality, local produce and the menus are excellent value. For 65 F, for example, you may enjoy such local foods as *toast au Maroilles*, *salade de chèvre chaude* or *terrine maison* followed by homemade *potjevleesch*, creamy, gelatinous *carbonnade de bœuf* braised slowly in dark beer, or tasty, free-range *poulet de Licques à la bière blonde*. For dessert, don't miss the *sorbet au genièvre de Houlle*, made from the local Dutch-style gin.

Closed Wed. and Jan. ❖ No credit cards ❖ Menus: 65 F, 95 F, 115 F, 145 F

62000 ARRAS (PAS DE CALAIS) 🛒

Marché Thur., Sat., Sun.
Calais 112 km – Amiens 67 km – Lille 51 km

HOTEL-RESTAURANT

Hôtel de l'Univers
3, place de la Croix
Rouge
tel.: 21 71 34 01
fax: 21 71 41 42

Situated in the centre of the town on the site of a sixteenth-century Jesuit monastery, this 3-star hotel is one of the best in town, something of a long-standing Arras institution known and loved by many including the British officers who occupied the building during the war, many of whom still return each year with their children and grandchildren. Family-owned and run by Madame Rambaud under the direction of Monsieur Daniel Gilleron who has been here thirty years and speaks perfect English, this is a classically French provincial hotel in the best sense. There are thirty-three comfortable, individually and newly redecorated rooms including five with four-poster beds, all with private bath or shower, w.c., television and telephone, located around the pretty gardens in the old cloisters of the monastery.

The long, beamed dining room, with wood-effect panelling, tapestry-covered chairs, and tables with heavy cloths, napkins stiffly pressed, is spacious and correct but not overly precious or pretentious. Cooking is strictly traditional with menus which change each month and a *carte* which changes twice a year. There are some good local dishes, excellent *salades composées*, fish from Boulogne and, of course, the famous *andouillette d'Arras*, here cooked in

genièvre de Houlle and finished in *crème fraîche*. The wine list is interesting and reasonably priced.

Open all year ❖ Credit cards: Visa/ CB, Eurocard/Access, American Express ❖ Rooms: double 300–380 F, breakfast 40 F ❖ Menus: 90 F, 160 F, 210 F ❖ à la carte: about 250 F ❖ Parking ❖ English spoken ❖ L S H B

Hôtel de l'Univers, Arras

RESTAURANT

La Faisanderie
45, Grand' Place
tel.: 21 48 20 76
fax: 21 50 89 18

La Faisanderie, Arras

The Faisanderie is probably the best restaurant in Arras. It combines confidently both historic atmosphere and impeccably modern, regional cooking. The dining room is located in seventeenth-century, vaulted caves below the Grand' Place. Settle down here to enjoy the procession of delicious and delectable cuisine which emanates from Jean-Pierre Dargent's kitchen: impeccably prepared and well-presented, with a character true to the region, as in *fricassée de queue de langoustines et de girolles, noisettes d'agneau de lait de pays rôties à la fleur de thym*, or the remarkably flavoursome *crepinettes de pieds de cochon braisées* served with a *purée* of the delicious local butter beans *lingots de Nord*. There is an excellent selection of local and regional cheeses, desserts that are works of art, sinfully irresistible *mignardaises* to accompany coffee, plus good though pricey wines.

Closed Sun. evening, Mon., a fortnight in Feb., and three weeks in Aug. ❖ Credit cards: Visa/CB, Eurocard/Access, American Express, Diners ❖ Menus: 175 F, 255 F, 375 F ❖ à la carte: about 350 F ❖ English spoken

---

62179 AUDINGHEN (PAS DE CALAIS)
Calais 22 km – Boulogne-sur-Mer 18 km – Marquise 10 km

CHAMBRE D'HÔTE

La Maison de la Houve
tel.: 21 32 97 06
21 83 29 95

Madame Danel, an effusive and utterly charming lady, says that she would like her house to be known as *la maison de l'amitié* – the house of friendship. She bought this isolated, rural dwelling, located about 4 kilometres outside Audinghen on the road to Marquise, she says, for her own children. However, they are now grown up and have all

Maison de la Houve, Audinghen

moved away. So she converted the old farmhouse into seven individually decorated *chambres*, partly, she says, to fill the house with children again. The rooms, a few of which have private or semi-private facilities, are as flamboyant as Madame Danel with four-poster beds, drapery over the beds, books everywhere, flowers everywhere, toys and books for children everywhere. Breakfast is served at whatever hour you like until midday in a lovely room with panoramic views of the rolling countryside across to Cap Blanc-Nez.

Open all year ❖ Rooms: two persons 125–170 F including breakfast. Children free

---

HOTEL-RESTAURANT

2 km N.W. at Cap Gris Nez

Hôtel-Restaurant Les Mauves
Cap Gris Nez
tel.: 21 32 96 06

Cap Gris Nez is the point on the French mainland closest to England. Indeed, on a good day, you can see the Kent coast so clearly that you can even make out buildings. Yet in spite of its proximity to England, not to mention Calais and Boulogne, this remains a wild, still almost wholly unspoiled stretch of the coast, with lovely cliff walks.

The Hôtel Les Mauves dates from 1920 and for its entire existence it has been in the hands of the Cugny family. Today, three sisters run this quiet and well-kept hôtel-restaurant which has an atmosphere that can only be described as *vieille française* in the best sense: correct, *propre*, provincial. The hotel has sixteen tastefully and individually decorated rooms, mainly on the small side but most with full private facilities. There is one large family room with private bathroom.

The dining room is comfortable in a family style, the sort of place where most of the diners, you imagine, are on *demi-pension*. The restaurant serves *cuisine traditionelle* based primarily on seafood and shellfish. Dishes particularly worth singling out include *feuilleté au crabe*, *coquilles St-Jacques à la nage* and *lotte au poivre vert*. Everything, including the *pâtisseries*, is made on the premises.

Les Mauves,
Cap Gris Nez

Today Cap Gris Nez is so peaceful that it is hard to imagine how this essentially calm, rural world was turned upside down during the war. Madame Cugny remembers that the hotel was taken over by the Germans. 'Of course, it was the officers who were billeted here. They liked to live well,' she remembers wryly. Do the Germans return today? 'Oh yes, they come back each summer *"comme chez-eux"*. C'est *drôle*, n'est-ce pas ?'

Closed 15 Nov.–end of March
❖ Room: double 350–400 F, breakfast 32 F ❖ Menus: 100 F, 148 F, 210 F

RESTAURANT

La Sirène
Cap Gris Nez
tel.: 21 32 95 97

Located right on the coast, at the end of a short lane just below the dominant headland of Cap Gris Nez, this outstanding, family-run shellfish restaurant is the place to come for traditional fish menus as well as for great platters of *fruits de mer* or special treats like *homard grillé sauce corail*. For the freshness of its seafood, for its dramatic and lonely position, and for the efficient but nonetheless warm welcome of the Boulnoy family: the Sirène deserves a visit. The dining room overlooks the beach. Look out, therefore, for any Channel swimmers because Cap Gris Nez is the closest landfall from England and historically the swimmers have always made for here.

Closed Sun. evening all year; Mon. except July and Aug.; end of Dec.–early Feb. ❖ Credit cards: Visa/CB, Eurocard/Access ❖ Menus: 110 F, 195 F ❖ à la carte: about 200 F ❖ English spoken

62164 AUDRESSELLES (PAS DE CALAIS)

Calais 28 km – Boulogne-sur-Mer 15 km

RESTAURANT

Chez Mimi
rue Accary
tel.: 21 32 96 00

Audresselles has long been famous for its *moules* as well as for shellfish like *crabe* and *homard*. Come to this simple, low-lying, whitewashed, Flemish cottage, sit at wooden trestles amidst a rustic decor and enjoy steaming bowls of *moules* or *soupe de poissons*, then grilled fish, or the favourite seafood medley, *marmite de pêcheur*.

Open daily all year ❖ à la carte: about 120 F

59440 AVESNES-SUR-HELPE (NORD)

Marché Fri.
Calais 185 km – St-Quentin 67 km – Valenciennes 41 km

FERME AUBERGE

8 km S. at Etrœungt

Ferme Auberge de La Capelette
Lieu dit La Capelette
tel.: 27 59 28 33
fax: 27 59 28 72

It is not all that easy to find the little hamlet of La Capelette located outside the small village of Etrœungt, not far from the hardly large market town of Avesnes-sur-Helpe: this is deepest rural France, after all, far from the madding crowd, the noise and traffic of cities, the realities of the twentieth century.

Here, Monsieur and Madame Delmée, a young couple with a young family, have created an impressive, purpose-built farmhouse restaurant which has proved to be extremely popular with locals from the surrounding countryside as well as with Belgians who come here by the coachload. Here, in a large, although admittedly not very atmospheric, dining room that is well suited to groups, you can enjoy the real foods of the Avesnois. The Delmées cultivate fine *pleurotte* and *shitaake* mushrooms on the farm. These are used extensively in the kitchen together with other fresh, local produce and products from their own and

The Avesnois

neighbouring farms. A typical weekday meal might start with homemade *rillettes* accompanied by a house *apéritif*, followed by *flamiche aux poireaux* or *feuilleté de pleurottes à la crème* hot from the oven, then a main course such as *pintadeau au hydromel* served with fresh garden vegetables, next a platter of local cheeses including, of course, Maroilles, Boulette d'Avesnes and Dauphin, and finally a homemade fruit *tarte*. Meals are accompanied by home-produced *cidre* or apple juice, Belgium beers or a selection of reasonably priced house wines.

Open middays and Sat. evening. Closed all day Wed. Reservations preferred
❖ No credit cards ❖ Menu: 100 F

59380 BERGUES (NORD)
Calais 50 km – Dunkerque 9 km

HOTEL-RESTAURANT

Au Tonnelier
4, rue du Mont de Piété
tel.: 28 68 70 05
fax: 28 68 21 87

Bergues, located just inland from Dunkerque, is an old fortified town rich in history, with part of the town fortifications still intact. This is a quiet, lovely corner of the Nord, and the town makes a pleasant base for excursions across the border into Belgium and exploration of Flandres-Maritime. There are eleven extremely clean if unstylish, 2-star rooms at the Tonnelier, not particularly large but each with its own shower, w.c., television and telephone. The large, traditional dining room is noted locally for its superlative, regional foods and, indeed, the restaurant has won awards for its version of the local speciality, *potjevleesch*, an ample cold terrine of chunks of chicken, rabbit, veal and pork set in a sharp, vinegary jelly, served usually with *pommes frites* and salad. Otherwise, the cuisine is ample and strictly *bourgeoise*; a typical 130 F menu might start with *terrine de foie de volaille*, followed by *langue de veau*, next the *chariot des fromages*, and finally a homemade dessert.

Closed Thur.; 19 Aug.–6 Sept. ❖ Credit cards: Visa/CB, Eurocard/Access ❖ Rooms: double 280 F, breakfast 28 F ❖ Menus: 78F, 93 F, 130 F, menu enfant 60 F ❖ à la carte: about 150 F ❖ English spoken

---

59299 BOESCHEPE (NORD)
Calais 76 km – Hazebrouck 16 km – Poperinge 6 km

ESTAMINET
BEER TAVERN

De Vierpot
125, rue du Moulin
tel.: 28 49 46 37

Notwithstanding that this *estaminet* beside Boeschepe's famous windmill may be a modern reproduction of the typical Flemish drinking taverns of *autrefois*, the Vierpot should on no account be missed if you find yourself anywhere near the Mont des Cats. This area, in any case, seems to have been almost by-passed by time, and in the Vierpot, Jean Maris, the young owner, has faithfully recreated an atmosphere which really does seem almost from another century. *Estaminets* typically served as the focal point of Flemish communities, places to enjoy simple foods, a game of cards and, of course,

a pot or two of the superlative, local brews. This tavern serves those same purposes today.

This is a good place to visit to sample an impressive range of local, artisan-brewed beers and Belgian beers, accompanied by the simplest drinking snacks.

De Vierpot,
Boeschepe

Closed Mon. ❖ Credit cards: Visa/CB, Eurocard/Access ❖ A little English spoken

62200 BOULOGNE-SUR-MER (PAS DE CALAIS) 🛒

Marché   Wed., Sat.
Calais 34 km – Le Touquet 32 km

HOTEL

Hôtel Métropole
51, rue Thiers
tel.: 21 31 54 30
fax: 21 30 45 72

Boulogne, quite frankly, does not overwhelm you with choices of nice places to stay. The Métropole is an old and reliable stand-by, located near the port in the heart of the principal shopping district. Boulogne's only 3-star hotel has some twenty-five spacious rooms, freshly decorated, each equipped with private bath or shower, w.c., television, telephone and mini-bar. There is a rather charming, flowered rear garden room where breakfast is served in fine weather.

Closed 20 Dec.–5 Jan. ❖ Credit cards: Visa/CB, Eurocard/Access, American Express, Diners ❖ Rooms: double 390 F, breakfast 40 F ❖ English spoken

HOTEL

Hôtel de Lorraine
7, place de Lorraine
tel.: 21 31 34 78

Good, clean, unpretentious accommodation is always welcome, so this small, 2-star hotel is a useful find. There are twenty rooms, though only eight have private facilities. While it has no restaurant, this is hardly a problem as its central location puts it within easy walking distance of a good many, including the always popular l'Huitrière which is almost next door.

Open all year ❖ Credit cards: Visa/CB, Eurocard/Access ❖ Rooms: 195–245 F, breakfast 28 F

CHAMBRE D'HÔTE

Mme Delabie
26, rue Flahaut
tel.: 21 31 88 74

Just outside the ramparts of Boulogne's atmospheric Haute-Ville, Madame Delabie offers five comfortable, nicely furnished *chambres* in her old, family house. Though only one room has private facilities, all the rooms are quite spacious and comfortable and there are a couple of modern shower rooms. Two rooms in the upstairs attic are adjoining and would be good for a family. What really makes this a special place is the personal welcome of Madame Delabie. She is extremely thoughtful and sensitive to the needs of her guests and genuinely wants to make them feel at home. If, for example, one morning you don't particularly want to breakfast early, no matter: she will serve it at whatever time

you get up, within reason. *'Ce n'est pas l'armée,'* she says – after all, this isn't the Army.

Rooms: two persons 250–350 F including breakfast

Haute-Ville, Boulogne-sur-Mer

RESTAURANT

La Matelote
80, boulevard Ste Beuve
tel.: 21 30 17 97
fax: 21 83 29 24

We consider Tony Lestienne's restaurant, located in front of Nausicaa and the Boulogne harbour, to be just about the best in town. The dining room is airy and fresh and the cooking is similarly like a breath of sea air. The *carte*, naturally, makes great use of the superlative seafood and shellfish of Boulogne. Witness the purity of *les noix de St-Jacques cuites à l'assiette au naturel* or *le blanc de turbot poché au marinière de moules* which we enjoyed on a recent visit. Yet other local and regional foods are not eschewed either: *volailles de Licques sauce crème aux morilles* is one regional dish which should not be missed. Excellent cheeses and homemade *pâtisseries* as well as some good, reasonably priced wines round off a satisfying dining experience.

Closed Sun. evening ❖ Credit cards: Visa/CB, Eurocard/Access ❖ Menus: 160 F, 210 F, 345 F ❖ à la carte: about 240–300 F ❖ English spoken

---

RESTAURANT IN THE
*CENTRE NATIONAL
DE LA MER*

**Restaurant de
Nausicaa**
Centre National de la
Mer
tel.: 21 33 24 24

Eurodisney take note: when the hugely impressive and dynamic *Centre national de la mer* opened just a few years ago, it made sure that the restaurant on site did justice to its celebration of the sea. Accordingly, rather than merely install an indifferent museum 'caff' catering to captive visitors and tourists, a serious restaurant worth visiting in its own right was created.

Only the French, after all, would, after touring this fascinating aquarium complex, find themselves feeling hungry for fish! Nausicaa is ultramodern in design and concept and the dining room of the restaurant benefits accordingly, with tall windows which overlook Boulogne's beach, and an airy, spacious feel that is most relaxing. Naturally, the foods on offer are almost entirely seafood orientated. Local mussels are served in five different ways. There is always a good selection of *huîtres*, *plateaux de fruits de mer* and the like, and there are also some good, local specialities which are always available, such as *choucroute de poissons* and *gainée boulonnaise*. The menus are good value and there are some reasonable wines on offer too.

In the adjoining bar, after visiting the museum, if you don't feel like a full meal, you can enjoy a *dégustation* of three *huîtres* together with a large glass of Alsatian wine for 25 F.

Open daily midday and evening ❖ Credit cards: Visa/CB, Eurocard/Access, American Express, Diners ❖ Menus: 78 F, 110 F, 145 F, 210 F, menu enfant 45 F ❖ à la carte: about 200 F ❖ English spoken

---

RESTAURANT

L'Huîtrière

11, place de Lorraine
tel.: 21 31 35 27

This tiny but stylish restaurant hides behind its *poissonnerie* shop front on a little square off the rue Faidherbe. There are only seven tables so it is all a bit cheek by jowl but this really is an excellent fish restaurant. Indeed, how Philippe Cardon manages to produce such a full and excellent range of foods from his tiny kitchen the size of a broom cupboard we don't know, but everything is always excellent (though service can be somewhat slow since it is virtually a one-man operation). Come here to enjoy huge *plateaux de fruits de mer*, super oysters, of course, (both *fines de claires* and *spéciales*), *feuilleté de moules au safron*, *gainée boulonnaise*, *assiette de pêcheur*, *waterzooï* and other hearty and substantial, fishy main courses followed by good, simple desserts and excellent coffee. The wine list is unambitious but reliable.

All of the seafood comes from the *poissonnerie* which fronts it: this itself is a useful outlet for shellfish or fish to take away.

Closed Sun. evening, Mon. ❖ Credit cards: Visa/CB, Eurocard/Access, American Express ❖ Menu: 120 F ❖ à la carte: about 200 F ❖ English spoken

RESTAURANT

Aux Pêcheurs d'Etaples

31, Grande Rue

tel.: 21 30 29 29

Any fish restaurant with an impressive and extensive *poissonnerie* fronting it naturally gains a certain street credibility, all the more so when it turns out that both establishments are run by a cooperative of fishermen. Thus, just opposite the Église St-Nicolas and Boulogne's principal Place Dalton, Aux Pêcheurs d'Etaples, a *poissonnerie*-restaurant run by the *Coopérative maritime étaploise*, serves as a showcase for its fishermen's superlative efforts.

In truth, though the raw ingredients are undoubtedly first class, we have found the cooking here to be pretty

uninspired. However, if you stick to basics you won't go far wrong. It is hard to beat the sumptuous *plateaux de fruits de mer* (with or without lobster), while other simple seafood classics are always satisfying: a richly concentrated *soupe de poissons*, simple, grilled fish, succulent *moules marinières*. The *poisson du jour* is almost always worth trying.

Open daily midday and evening ❖ Credit cards: Visa/CB, Eurocard/Access, American Express, Diners ❖ Menus: 100F, 130 F, menu enfant 40 F ❖ à la carte: about 160–200 F

Aux Pêcheurs d'Etaples, Boulogne-sur-Mer

BAR-*BRASSERIE*

Bar-Brasserie Hamiot

1, rue Faidherbe

tel.: 21 31 44 20

Come to this bar-*brasserie*, perennially popular with the fishermen, from 0600 for a hearty breakfast of *bacon, œufs et frites*, or later in the day, sit out in the sun and nurse a beer or two accompanied by a steaming bowl of *moules-frites*. Bar Hamiot is something of an institution, not only for the locals themselves but for scores of British visitors and day-trippers who make this their first port of call after stepping off the

Seacat or ferry. For all that, it is a serious alternative for those in search of good, honest foods, simply prepared and speedily served. There is always a *plat du jour – veau à la provençale, couscous, marmite de pêcheur* – and the menus are reliable.

Open daily ❖ Menus: 95 F, 150 F, plat du jour 45 F, menu enfant 40 F ❖ à la carte: about 80–150 F

62100 CALAIS (PAS DE CALAIS) 🛒

Marché Wed., Sat.
Boulogne-sur-Mer 34 km – Dunkerque 45 km – St-Omer 46 km

HOTEL-RESTAURANT

Le George V
36, rue Royale
tel.: 21 97 68 00
fax: 21 97 34 73

If you want to stay in Calais, the George V is hard to beat. The hotel is centrally located in the heart of Calais Nord, just a few paces from the Place d'Armes along the town's best shopping artery. This 3-star *Logis de France* has forty-three sound-proofed rooms all with private facilities, French and English television, telephone and mini-bar, and there is secure parking at the back. Best of all, the hotel has two fine restaurants, Le Petit George and the Restaurant George V, divided in the same room by a cloth screen. The Petit is decidely less formal, popular not just with English guests but also with Calaisien families, and the food is good. The two-course 65 F menu, for example, offers a choice of

Calais

eight first courses including *salade licquoise, terrine de lapin, soupe de poissons,* and eight main courses which include *lapin à la dijonaise, choucroute de poissons, coq à la bière de garde.* Cheese and desserts are extra. The Restaurant George V is a little more formal, though by no means overly so, the tables laid with porcelain dishes and crystal wine goblets; the food, too, is more considered, less family-style, with a 155 F *menu du jour* that includes local oysters and seafood as well as regional dishes such as *fricassée de poulet de Licques aux langoustines,* an excellent selection of local and regional cheeses and some delectable *pâtisseries maisons.*

Bernard Beauvolot, who comes from a family of brewers, is a most genial host and he is more than happy to direct his English clientèle to the main points of interest in Calais.

Hotel open all year. Restaurant closed Sat. midday, Sun. evening ❖ Credit cards: Visa/CB, Eurocard/Access, American Express, Diners ❖ Rooms: double 220–360 F, buffet breakfast 38 F ❖ Menus: 65–250 F, menu enfant available ❖ à la carte: 110–250 F ❖ Parking ❖ English, German and Dutch spoken ❖ L S H B

HOTEL

Hôtel Windsor

2, rue du Commandant Bonningue

tel.: 21 34 59 40

fax: 21 97 68 59

This small, somewhat eccentric hotel near the Place d'Armes and opposite the *phare* is popular and always busy. It is owned and run by M. and Mme de Molay. There are fifteen rooms, eleven of which have private facilities; though they are traditionally furnished and nothing special in themselves, they are impeccably well kept and spotless with a close attention to every detail, from the way the beds are turned down at night to the thick towels, bathrobes, and the sweets that are placed in each room every night. The 'Wimbledon' room sleeps four and is ideal for families. There is a secure, private garage.

Open all year ❖ Credit cards: Visa/CB, Eurocard/Access, American Express, Diners ❖ Rooms: double 225–245 F, breakfast 28 F ❖ Parking ❖ English spoken

Small Hotels and Restaurants

RESTAURANT

Le Channel
3, boulevard de la
Résistance
tel.: 21 34 42 30
fax: 21 97 42 43

Monsieur and Madame Crespo's popular restaurant opposite Calais's *port de plaisance* is rated by many as the best fish restaurant in town and we would not disagree. The raw ingredients are virtually straight off the boats and the cooking, though not innovative, is solid and traditional. We suggest that you stick to the classics – *turbot poché sauce hollandaise, les noix de St-Jacques aux légumes, bar grillé* – and you won't go far wrong. There is an excellent selection of cheeses from the Maison du Fromage. The menus are good value.

Closed Tue., Sun. evening ❖ Credit cards: Visa/CB, Eurocard/Access, American Express, Diners ❖ Menus: 85 F, 135 F, 190 F, 300 F (including wine) ❖ à la carte: about 250 F ❖ English and Spanish spoken

---

RESTAURANT

La Sole Meunière
1, boulevard de la
Résistance
tel.: 21 34 43 01
fax: 21 97 65 62

Also located by the waterfront, next door to Le Channel, La Sole Meunière naturally specializes in seafood as well, served outdoors at pavement tables in summer, in the bright, airy dining room with views of the ferries at other times. Chef Christophe Langlais has been here five years and he prepares his foods with some imagination. The *carte*, for example, offers *coquilles St-Jacques* in ten different ways. There are regional dishes like *marmite calaisienne* (a hearty sort of seafood medley) and *boudin de poisson blanc aux lentilles vertes*. And for those with a sweet tooth, there is a *menu pâtisserie* which includes a vast selection of *pâtisseries* and *sorbets*, accompanied by a bottle of house Champagne.

Closed Mon. ❖ Credit cards: Visa/CB, Eurocard/Access, American Express, Diners ❖ Menus: 80 F, 120 F, 160 F, 250 F ❖ à la carte: about 150–200 F ❖ English spoken

---

CAFÉ-RESTAURANT-
BRASSERIE

Au Moniteur
5 et 7, place d'Armes
tel.: 21 34 50 14

'On mange bien au Moniteur,' the locals advised us. This city centre café-restaurant on the main Place d'Armes, in truth, is nothing particularly special. However, it is traditional, inexpensive and, most important in this town which at times seems to cater almost exclusively for its English visitors, wholly and authentically French. Come here simply for a sandwich and a glass of beer, for a single *plat du jour* or for one of the simple, inexpensive menus – *assiette de crudités,*

potage du jour, sole meunière, fromage – and enjoy *la différence*.

Closed Tue. evening out of season, Wed. all year ❖ Credit cards: Visa/ CB, Eurocard/Access, American Express, Diners ❖ Menus: 65 F, 80 F, 120 F ❖ à la carte: about 80–120 F ❖ English spoken

Market, Place d'Armes, Calais

59400 CAMBRAI (NORD) 🛒

Marché Daily except Mon.

Calais 150 km – Arras 36 km – Lille 64 km

HOTEL-RESTAURANT

Hostellerie Château de la Motte Fénelon

allée St-Roch
BP 174
tel.: 27 83 61 38
fax: 27 83 71 61

This beautiful and elegant château hotel located just outside town on its northern edge, set within its own 8-hectare parkland, comes as something of a peaceful relief after the hustle and bustle of the Cambrai town centre. The nineteenth-century mansion was built by a local laundryman who made a fortune on the back of the town's once thriving textile industry. He built this grandiose château to prove to the local aristocracy that he had made it but it is our guess that they probably still thought of him as 'trade'. During both world wars, it was occupied by the Germans, eventually abandoned and left in ruins.

Today, phoenix-like, the Château de la Motte Fénelon has been restored to its former glory and must certainly rate as one of the finest hotels in the area. There are forty rooms in all, the best of which are located in both the château itself

Château de la Motte Fénelon, Cambrai

as well as in the newly renovated 'Orangerie' stable block. Furthermore, within the grounds of the park, there are some twenty-two motel-style bungalows, perhaps a little dated now and certainly more modest in decor and feel but convenient for families, reasonably priced and excellent value. Each room including those in the bungalows has private bath, w.c., television, telephone and mini-bar.

The hotel boasts an excellent and atmospheric restaurant, Les Douves, located in the brick, vaulted cellars below the château. This is a warm, elegant place for a romantic dinner by candlelight and the cuisine, if not exceptional, is worthy of the lovely setting. Specialities include *marbre de foie gras d'oie, poêlée d'escargots au beurre, magret de canard grillé au beurre d'herbes fines*. Service is correct but not overly formal. While wines tend to be rather pricey, the best buy is Château Barateau, an outstanding, mature claret from a property in the Haut-Médoc under the same ownership as the hotel.

Sports facilities include a tennis court, fitness centre, billiards table and table tennis.

Closed Sun. evening ❖ Credit cards: Visa/CB, Eurocard/Access, American Express, Diners ❖ Rooms: double in château or Orangerie 440–540 F, suite in château 950–1000 F, double in bungalow 290 F, buffet breakfast 50 F ❖ Menus: 140 F, 190 F, 225 F ❖ à la carte: about 300 F ❖ English spoken

RESTAURANT-
RÔTISSERIE

L'Escargot

10, rue Général de
Gaulle
tel.: 27 81 24 54
fax: 27 83 95 21

This typically Cambresian eating house, located just off the main town square, is the place to come to sample the town's great speciality, *andouillette de Cambrai*. Guy Maton makes his own, utilizing exclusively *fraise de veau*, and will cook it in front of you over a charcoal fire in the ground-floor dining room. Enjoy this simple but delicious speciality as well as other typical *charcuterie* products such as *boudin noir sucré* served with a compote of apples, good, grilled steaks and fish.

Closed Mon., Wed. evening ❖ Credit cards: Visa/CB, Eurocard/Access, American Express, Diners ❖ Menus: 75 F, 110 F, 220 F ❖ à la carte: about 150 F

62240 DESVRES (PAS DE CALAIS)

Marché Tue.
Calais 40 km – Boulogne-sur-Mer 16 km

RESTAURANT

Café Jules

11, place Léon Blum
tel.: 21 91 69 72

If you come to Desvres to see, learn about and purchase faïence pottery, the Café Jules, located on the huge, central market square, is a useful place to stop for lunch. This simple, unpretentious and wholly authentic restaurant serves mainly a local clientèle who appreciate good, home-cooked foods dished up in generous proportions. Come here for reliable, unchanging classics such as homemade *terrines*, *coq à la bière*, *carbonnade flamande* and monthly specials like *couscous* served on the first Wednesday of every month, *la tête de veau* served on the second, *paëlla* on the third, and *cassoulet* on the fourth.

Open middays only except for groups by reservation. Closed Sat., two weeks in Feb., two weeks in Sept. ❖ Credit cards: Visa/CB, Eurocard/Access ❖ Menus: 85 F (weekdays only), 125 F

Small Hotels and Restaurants

59140 DUNKERQUE (NORD) 🛒

Marché Wed., Sat.
Calais 45 km — Oostende 55 km

HOTEL-RESTAURANT

*6 km S.E. at
Téteghem*

La Meunerie
174, rue des Pierres
tel.: 28 26 01 80
fax: 28 26 17 32

Monsieur and Madame Jean-Pierre Delbé came to this old, steam-powered millhouse in 1971. They transformed it first into one of the greatest restaurants in the region and now into a luxury hotel-restaurant with nine superior rooms which must rate as one of the most desirable places in the Nord for a special weekend away.

Téteghem, in truth, is in the middle of nowhere, located just outside Dunkerque towards the Belgium frontier. But the Meunerie definitely deserves a visit. The 4-star bedrooms are located in an annexe attached to the millhouse restaurant by a futuristic, glassed-in corridor. All nine are really special, spacious with either balconies or terraces on to the garden, luxuriously appointed with beautiful, marble bathrooms and decorated in styles that range from the traditional to the ultramodern: naturally they have all those extras that you expect in a hotel of this class.

But it should be said that one comes to the Meunerie primarily to eat. This is indeed one of the great restaurants of the Nord, perhaps of northern France. As in all great restaurants, what makes it so very special is the owner's almost manic obsession with even the tiniest detail, the elegant table settings, Cristophle silver and crystal stemware, fresh flowers, the nibbles offered with drinks, the homemade breads and sweet, unsalted butter, the extra courses slipped in between main courses, the young, unfussy service, the *carte des vins* and impeccable wine service. All this is combined with cuisine that is light, elegant yet substantial, perfectly balanced and full of delightful, fresh flavours. Dishes we enjoyed include *huîtres tièdes au sabayon de Champagne, duo de raie et dorade dans un coulis d'herbes, l'agneau à l'épeautre de saulx*, and delightful desserts such as *mousse de pistache et glace de vanille* and *croustillant de pommes caramelisées au glace de miel.*

Breakfast is served in either the dining room or your bedroom and is also superlative: freshly squeezed juice, fresh fruit salad, home-baked *viennoiserie* which includes beautiful, buttery *croissants* and rich, yeasty *brioches* still warm from the oven, homemade fruit *confitures*, individual *crème brulée*, *fromage blanc*, and cereals.

Throughout the year, Madame Delbé offers special *'forfait weekend'* inclusive tariffs which include a double bedroom for Saturday night, dinner Saturday evening, breakfast and a light Sunday lunch. Telephone or fax for current details.

Closed Sun. evening, Mon., 20 Dec.–10 Jan. ❖ Credit cards: Visa/ CB, Eurocard/Access, Diners ❖ Rooms: double 450–800 F, suite 1,350 F, breakfast 70 F ❖ Menus: 250 F, 300 F (*menu surprise* including *apéritif*, wine and coffee), 380 F, 450 F ❖ à la carte: about 550 F ❖ Parking ❖ English spoken

La Meunerie, Téteghem

62179 ESCALLES (PAS DE CALAIS)
Calais 10 km – Boulogne-sur-Mer 27 km

RESTAURANT

Restaurant du Cap
place de la Mairie
tel.: 21 85 25 10
fax: 21 36 12 83

The Cap has been adopted as the favourite 'local' by many Eurotunnel employees ensconced at nearby Coquelles, and a number of them have praised it highly to us. Indeed, the proximity of this excellent and popular restaurant to the Channel Tunnel Terminal, near the dramatic headland of Cap Blanc Nez, should make it a popular destination for the rest of us, too. The long, rustic-style main dining room is fairly informal, the atmosphere warm and easy; in summer you can enjoy drinks outside on the garden terrace. Come to the Cap to *déguster* excellent and always extremely fresh seafood and shellfish. The *plateaux de fruits de mer* are impeccably fresh and generous and there are always good, sea-fresh oysters and mussels available as well as live lobsters from the *vivier*. The specialities of chef Pierre Stival also include *cassolette de noix St-Jacques aux champignons*, *brochette de saumon* and *le gigot d'agneau rôti aux chevriers verts*. The Cap is popular with groups and always full at Sunday lunchtimes, so it is advisable to book.

Open middays daily and Sat. evening out of season; open middays and evenings daily July–Aug. ❖ Credit cards: Visa/CB, Eurocard/Access, American Express, Diners ❖ Menus: 114 F, 132 F, 146 F, 185 F, menu enfant 50 F ❖ à la carte: about 135–200 F ❖ English spoken

---

CHAMBRE D'HÔTE

La Grand' Maison
Haute-Escalles
tel.: 21 85 27 75

Those who might hesitate to experience French *chambres d'hôtes* should certainly consider visiting La Grand' Maison, located just 5 kilometres from the Channel Tunnel in peaceful, rural country in sight of the sea. Here, Jacqueline and Marc Boutroy have created a quite welcoming and lovely, little operation centred around their traditional, working farmhouse. The couple now offer six beautiful, large and newly renovated *chambres*, all individually decorated and with good, modern facilities including private shower and w.c. for each room. These rooms, quite frankly, are of a standard that is higher than that found in many small hotels. A few of the newly converted rooms are located in the old stable; those on the first floor are reached by a very steep staircase which might not be suitable for young children or the elderly. The Boutroys also have two *gîtes ruraux* available for rent by the week or longer.

Open all year ❖ Rooms: two persons 190–250 F, three persons 260–350 F including breakfast ❖ A little English spoken

62630 ETAPLES (PAS DE CALAIS) 🛒
Marché   Tue., Fri.
Calais 58 km – Montreuil-sur-Mer 11 km – Boulogne-sur-Mer 27 km

RESTAURANT

**Aux Pêcheurs
d'Etaples**
quai de la Canche
tel.: 21 94 06 90

*Soupe de poissons,
Aux Pêcheurs
d'Etaples, Etaples*

Aux Pêcheurs d'Etaples is the original restaurant of the *Coopérative maritime étaploise* (there are also branches in Boulogne-sur-Mer and Lille) with the now familiar formula of an outstanding *poissonnerie* fronting, in this case, an excellent, first-floor restaurant. This popular and well-known establishment stands just behind the fishermen's *quai*, the boats of the fleet bobbing up and down on the tide. Don't come here, though, expecting some rough-and-ready fisherman's shack. The restaurant is a large and very professional operation with a comfortable, light, first-floor dining room, efficient, friendly service and a pleasant, informal atmosphere. The cooking here is better than in its sister establishment at Boulogne but this is still the place to come to enjoy essentially simple foods: rich, concentrated *soupe de poissons, la salade de poissons fumés au beurre blanc,*

always excellent *huîtres* and *moules*, *bouillabaise étaploise* and, of course, superlative and sumptious *plateaux de fruits de mer*. Indeed, it is the latter which the French themselves come here almost exclusively to enjoy, and on a weekend lunchtime, the dining room resounds to the cracking of crab claws and the enjoyable hum of slurping and sucking as every morsel of *langoustines*, crab legs, tiny sea snails and whelks, oysters and mussels is efficiently and impressively dispatched.

Open daily, closed Jan. ❖ Credit cards: Visa/CB, Eurocard/Access, American Express, Diners ❖ Menus: 100 F, 130 F, menu enfant 40 F ❖ à la carte: about 200 F ❖ English spoken

---

62310 FRUGES (PAS DE CALAIS) 🍴
Calais 65 km – St-Omer 55 km – Hesdin 20 km

FERME AUBERGE
AND CHEESE DAIRY

7 km S. at Créquy

Sire de Créquy
route de Créquy
tel.: 21 90 60 24
fax: 21 86 27 72

Sunday is the day to come to a *ferme auberge*. This is because the best, like Sire de Créquy, are popular with country folk from the surrounding area. Sunday, after all, is the farmer's day of rest and there is a long-standing tradition of enjoying big family meals at midday. Thus at *fermes auberges* special menus are often offered that seem almost endless.

A Sunday meal here is indeed impressive and you should ensure that you arrive suitably famished. A typical *repas* starts with a homemade *apéritif* of *liqueur de noix* accompanied by nibbles of small, fresh cheese cubes. Then a large bowl of *rillettes de canard* might be served followed by the famous and obligatory *flamiche au fromage*, served piping hot from the oven and made, of course, with the distinctive and flavoursome Sire de Créquy cheese. Next comes the main course, perhaps something simple and traditional like *poulet aux champignons*, served with home-conserved *haricots verts* and potatoes fried in duck fat. A pear sorbet drenched in liqueur serves as something of a local *trou*. Then the real *pièce de résistance*: a whole Sire de Créquy cheese per table, more bread, and a pot of *fromage aux fines herbes*, the fresh *fromage blanc* macerated with garlic, pepper and herbs. Next comes a pot of creamy farmhouse yoghurt sweetened with sugar. And finally, just in case anyone is still hungry (most seem to be), a warm slice of *tarte à la crème aux raisins*.

Afterwards, if you can still move, ask to tour the cheese dairy and *cave d'affinage*.

Open daily except Mon. all year round. Reservations essential weekends and advisable at other times. Group visits welcome by reservation (20–150 persons). ❖ Credit cards: Visa/CB, Eurocard/Access ❖ Menus: 60 F, 75 F, 100 F, 110 F ❖ A little English spoken

---

59570 GUSSIGNIES (NORD) 🚍

Calais 189 km – Valenciennes 28 km – Bavay 7 km

CAFÉ-RESTAURANT
AND ARTISAN
BREWERY

**Café-Restaurant-
Brasserie Au Baron**

place des Rocs
tel.: 27 66 88 61

During the week, Alain Bailleux spends most of his time brewing the distinctive range of Au Baron beers in tiny batches in this fascinating *boutique* brewery. At weekends, he has the pleasure of serving almost all of his production to appreciative French and Belgian customers who descend on this idyllic spot just kilometres from the frontier.

This is a particularly congenial, if out of the way, place to come, whether simply to sit outside on the terrace beside the babbling River Hogneau enjoying a Champagne-size bottle of the distinctive, rich, artisan-brewed beer together with a plate of Maroilles cheese, or to enjoy a full meal in the always crowded restaurant at weekends. Here Bailleux has converted an old brewing copper into an indoor grill

*Au Baron,
Gussignies*

where he cooks meats (steaks, brochettes, chops, *magret de canard*) and fish (trout and salmon) over an open fire, the sappy taste of wood going particularly well with the rich, distinctive flavours of the home-brewed beers.

In summer, the café is open every afternoon except Wednesdays and serves the full range of beers (*blonde, ambrée, brune*) with simple drinking snacks including *assiette campagnarde, tarte au Maroilles, escaveche*, sandwiches and tarts.

Café and Restaurant open Fri. evening–Sun. all year. In July and Aug. only the café is open daily from 1500, except Wed. Beers can be purchased at the adjoining brewery daily except Wed. during working hours. Reservations for meals advisable. ❖ Credit card: Visa/CB ❖ à la carte: about 150 F ❖ English spoken

---

62152 HARDELOT (PAS DE CALAIS)
Calais 47 km – Le Touquet 25 km – Boulogne-sur-Mer 15 km

HOTEL-RESTAURANT

Hôtel du Parc
111, avenue
François 1er
tel.: 21 33 22 11
fax: 21 83 29 71

This modern sports complex and hotel is an ideal place to come for a short, active break. As part of the Domaine de Hardelot, guests have access to two championship, eighteen-hole golf courses. Leisure facilities in the hotel itself include an outdoor, heated swimming pool, five tennis courts (indoor and all-weather), sauna, snooker tables, games room, fitness centre, and volleyball and basketball courts. Additional activities which can be arranged by the hotel include horse riding, windsurfing and sand yachting. There are plenty of good walks along the extensive beach and sand dunes.

The Parc, opened in 1992 by Prince Edward, is a well-appointed, modern, 3-star hotel. The eighty-one rooms are spacious, each furnished with two double beds, a small terrace, private bathroom and w.c., satellite television, telephone and mini-bar. The hotel bar is extremely popular with golfers. Meals are served in the large, informal Orangerie *brasserie*, primarily hearty and typical *bistro* foods such as *choucroute royale, tête de veau, bœuf gros sel, confit de canard* plus a selection of daily fresh fish and shellfish and a *plat du jour*. In fine weather during the season, buffet and barbeque meals are served outdoors on the terrace around the swimming pool.

*Hôtel du Parc,
Hardelot*

Closed 19 Dec.–19 Jan. ❖ Credit cards: Visa/CB, Eurocard/Access, American Express, Diners ❖ Rooms: double 390–590 F, breakfast 50 F ❖ Menu: 130 F, menu enfant 50 F ❖ à la carte: 130–150 F ❖ English and German spoken ❖ L S H B

BAR-*BRASSERIE*-RESTAURANT

L'Océan
100, boulevard de la Mer
tel.: 21 83 17 98

This well-situated bar-*brasserie* on Hardelot's seafront is the place to visit for *un demi* or a *citron pressé* perhaps accompanied by a dozen *huîtres* or a fresh seafood platter. Enjoy simple snacks or fishy menus on the terrace in summer or in the light and airy interior while watching the windsurfers and sand yachts.

Closed Tue. out of season; Jan. ❖ Credit cards: Visa/CB, Eurocard/Access ❖ Menus: 105 F, 145 F, menu enfant 50 F ❖ à la carte: about 100–150 F ❖ English spoken

---

62140 HESDIN (PAS DE CALAIS) 🛒

Marché Thur.

Calais 86 km – Montreuil-sur-Mer 25 km – Boulogne-sur-Mer 59 km

---

HOTEL-RESTAURANT-
RÔTISSERIE

**Hôtel-Restaurant-
Rôtisserie
Les Flandres**
20–22, rue d'Arras
tel.: 21 86 80 21
fax: 21 86 28 01

Hesdin

This family-run hotel-restaurant in the town centre has been in the hands of the Persyn family since about the turn of the century but the building has actually been a hotel since as long ago as 1598. Today there are fourteen rooms and they are all adequate if not exceptional. Those on the second floor have been pleasantly redecorated this year and each has private bath, w.c., television and telephone; those on the first floor are pleasant enough, too, though a little more dated in decor. The best feature here, though, is the long, rather old-fashioned, ground-floor dining room which, at its far end, has a gas *rôtisserie* where at both lunch and dinner a large joint of beef or lamb is cooked before the diners, the meat slowly rotating, its dripping juices adding a nice, warm scent to the room. The cuisine is traditional and regional, unfussy, copious and served in a pleasant and

informal atmosphere: no wonder, then, that the dining room is always full of locals as well as hotel guests. Some specialities include an outstanding fresh *table d'hors d'hœuvres*, homemade goose liver *pâté*, *coq à la bière*, *truite à la crème*, *saumon flamand*, *chaudière*, and, of course, meats cooked on the spit, served with *flageolets* and sautéed potatoes. There is an excellent selection of local cheeses including Sire de Créquy, Rollot and Trappe de Belval, and wines are fairly priced.

Closed 20 Dec.–10 Jan. ❖ Credit cards: Visa/CB, Eurocard/Access, American Express ❖ Rooms: double 260 F, buffet breakfast 35 F ❖ Menus: 75 F, 110 F, 180 F, menu enfant 45 F ❖ à la carte: about 150 F ❖ Parking ❖ English spoken

62170 INXENT (PAS DE CALAIS)
Calais 62 km – Boulogne-sur-Mer 32 km – Montreuil-sur-Mer 7 km

HOTEL-RESTAURANT

Auberge d'Inxent

318, rue de la Vallée
tel.: 21 90 71 19
fax: 21 86 31 67

The lovely valleys of the Boulonnais, such as the Canche, the Course, the Créquoise, and others, provide some of the most beautiful, idyllic, still wholly unspoiled country that we have encountered anywhere in the north of France. The Auberge d'Inxent, for example, located in the Vallée de la Course between Boulogne-sur-Mer and Montreuil, is a small, rustic hideaway of real peace and charm. Elizabeth David wrote lovingly about the inn some decades ago in her classic *French Provincial Cooking* and we imagine the place has changed little since then: modest, rustic, serving simple but outstanding foods based on the freshest country ingredients. Trout is the speciality of the house. When you order it, a kitchen minion is dispatched to the bottom of the garden where, in a stone *vivier* beside the fast-flowing Course, the fish is netted and brought back to be cooked to order, either *au bleu* or in the style of the *auberge*, with shallots, white wine and cream. Other simple classics include homemade *terrines*, *ficelle de l'auberge*, *poulet de la grande mère* and *tarte aux wambrechiés* (basically an apple tart flavoured with genièvre de Wambrechiés) served with farm-fresh cream.

There are six rooms in the *auberge*, all on the small side but beautifully furnished, bright and immaculate. Each has private bath or shower, w.c., television and telephone. Two rooms are adjoining and would suit a family.

Closed Tue. evening, Wed. out of season, 15 Dec.–20 Jan. ❖ Credit cards: Visa/CB, Eurocard/Access ❖ Rooms: double 350–400 F, breakfast 40 F ❖ Menus: 95 F, 120 F, 150 F, 250 F, menu enfant 60 F ❖ à la carte: about 150 F ❖ English spoken

Auberge d'Inxent, Inxent

59530 JOLIMETZ (NORD)
Calais 180 km – Valenciennes 18 km

RESTAURANT

Restaurant Le Grill de Mormal
29, rue du Pavé
tel.: 27 49 50 60
fax: 27 49 50 65

This old, country-style restaurant located in a small town on the edge of the extensive Fôret de Mormal has been beautifully converted and decorated by its new, young owner, Caroline Lust. The well-worn, quarry-tile floor, the huge, open fireplace, the original, beamed ceiling all remain, but the curtains are bright and fresh, the tables laid with some style and panache. Here, primarily simple foods – *salade de pays*, *feuilleté d'escargots*, grilled meats and fish – are presented with similar care and style and the cooking is well above average. Meals finish with sensational, home-baked fruit tarts.

Closed Tue. evening, Wed. ❖ Credit cards: Visa/CB, Eurocard/Access ❖ Menus: 72 F, 95 F, 160 F, 190 F ❖ à la carte: about 150–200 F ❖ English spoken

59287 LEWARDE (NORD)

Calais 135 km – Douai 10 km

RESTAURANT-
BRASSERIE IN CENTRE
HISTORIQUE MINIER

Le Briquet
Fosse Delloye
tel.: 27 98 03 89
fax: 27 96 18 31

The *Centre historique minier* draws over 100,000 visitors a year to the site of the former Delloye pit. Former miners guide visitors through the labour and life of the men and women who worked the, mine. This is an important and fascinating industrial centre and it is well worth a visit.

The miners themselves were only allowed twenty-five minutes to eat their meals underground. Visitors today, in typically French fashion, fare rather better. The restaurant-*brasserie*, a refurbished, old site canteen, is not bad at all and serves both snacks and *restauration rapide* as well as authentically prepared, regional foods including *coq à la bière du Ch'ti, flamiche au Maroilles, la ficelle picarde, carbonnade flamande, lapin aux pruneaux*. There is always a *plat du jour*.

Closed 1 Jan., 15–31 Jan., 1 May, 1 Nov., 25 Dec., and Mon. Oct.–Jan.
❖ Credit cards: Visa/CB, Eurocard/Access ❖ Menus: 74 F, 98 F, 128 F, 150 F, menu enfant 32 F, 42 F ❖ à la carte: about 120 F

62850 LICQUES (PAS DE CALAIS) 🛒

Marché Mon.
Festival *Fête de la Dinde* last two Mon. before Christmas
Calais 20 km – Ardres 10 km – St-Omer 20 km

FERME AUBERGE

6 km S. at Surques

Manoir du Brugnobois
205, route de Boulogne
tel.: 21 32 32 54

The Lorgnier family raise the famous *volailles de Licques* on their sprawling farm just south of the eponymous poultry centre and serve them with many other home-cooked, local foods in their welcoming, family-style farmhouse restaurant. Their great specialities are award-winning, homemade *terrines – terrine de volaille, terrine de lapin, rillettes d'oie –* and Ghislaine Lorgnier's homemade tarts such as the savoury, first-course *tourte au fromage*, or equally delicious desserts like the supremely simple *tarte à la crème*. In truth, the main courses are merely adequate although Sunday menus look more interesting. However, the prices are so reasonable, the welcome and service so genuine, we would gladly return here again. There is a good, limited wine list and passable house *cuvée* at 35 F a bottle.

After dining here, don't leave without purchasing a glass pot of *terrine de lapin* or *rillettes d'oie* together with a boxed *tourte* or *tarte*.

Open daily. Essential to reserve on Sun. ❖ Credit cards: Visa/CB, Eurocard/Access ❖ Menus: 50 F, 85 F, 120 F

FERME AUBERGE WITH
CHAMBRES D'HÔTE

*7 km S.E. at Bas
Loquin*

**Ferme Auberge des
Peupliers**

38, rue du Bas Loquin
Hameau du Bas-
Locquin
tel.: 21 39 63 70

If you, like us, love duck, it is well worth hunting out this *ferme auberge*. Monsieur and Madame Dusautoir specialize in the *élevage de canards* on their small farm, the products of which are served in this excellent, family-style farmhouse restaurant. The great speciality, of course, is superlative, home-produced and home-cooked *foie gras de canard* followed by *magret de canard*, *fromage de chèvre* and *tarte maison* (195 F menu). Other less exalted foods that can be enjoyed include *cou farci*, *rillettes de canard*, and *confit de canard*. In summer, you can eat outside in the front garden.

This is a true family operation, and almost all the foods served come from the farm. There are also four brand new *chambres* each with private shower and w.c. for visitors who care to stay on the farm. The entire process of raising the ducks can be witnessed and, of course, all the products of the farm are available for sale.

Closed Mon. Reservations preferable and advised on Sun. ❖ Credit card: Visa/CB ❖ Menus: 90 F, 119 F, 195 F ❖ Rooms: two persons 210 F including breakfast ❖ L S H B

59000 LILLE (NORD) 🚉

Marché Daily
Festival *La Braderie* first Sun. in Sept.
Calais 112 km – Brussels 116 km – Dunkerque 73 km

HOTEL

**Grand Hôtel
Bellevue**

5, rue Jean Roisin
tel.: 20 57 45 64
fax: 20 40 07 93

The Bellevue, located on Lille's central Grande Place in the heart of the city, is one of Lille's grand, old, traditional hotels and dates from the eighteenth century. The young Wolfgang Amadeus Mozart stayed here while on a European tour with his father.

Today, this long-established institution has some eighty 3-star rooms, each furnished in a different style ranging from traditional French provincial to Art Nouveau, from the rather dated but nostalgic style of the 1950s to the style of the 1990s. Most of the rooms are large, light, and luxuriously fitted; all benefit from soundproofing and each is well equipped

Grande Place, Lille

with large bathroom, w.c., television, telephone and mini-bar. Sixteen rooms overlook the Grande Place, each with its own tiny terrace on which you can stand and look out over the paved cafés and fountains of old Lille.

While the Bellevue does not have a restaurant, there is no shortage of good places to eat, while atmospheric Vieux Lille is just a few steps away. Also, *repas gastronomiques* (superior room service meals) including *foie gras frais* and *filet de bœuf grillé* are available.

Open all year ❖ Credit cards: Visa/CB, Eurocard/Access, American Express, Diners ❖ Rooms: double 495–760 F, buffet breakfast 60 F
❖ Nearby underground public parking
❖ English spoken ❖ L S H B

HOTEL

Hôtel Brueghel
5, parvis St-Maurice
tel.: 20 06 06 69
fax: 20 63 25 27

The Brueghel is one of the best centrally located, small, private, 2-star hotels that we found in Lille, and offers clean, adequate accommodation in seventy smallish, simply furnished rooms with some character, most of which have their own private bathroom, w.c., and telephone. Located off a pleasant pedestrian area between the Grande Place and the railway station, this is a nice, quiet place to stay; the best rooms overlook the Église St-Maurice.

Credit cards: Visa/CB, Eurocard/Access ❖ Rooms: double 250–300 F, breakfast 28 F ❖ Nearby underground parking

Small Hotels and Restaurants

HOTEL-RESTAURANT

Ibis Centre

avenue Ch. St-Venant
tel.: 20 55 44 44
fax: 20 31 06 25

There are times, especially on arriving in a new, large and somewhat intimidating city, when the anonymity of a chain hotel can be comforting. This centrally located, 2-star Ibis is a case in point. The hundred-plus rooms are all comfortably equipped with private facilities, and given the location, they are remarkably quiet. The location near the TGV *gare*, about ten minutes' walk from the Grande Place, is convenient and there is secure, underground parking attached to the hotel. The restaurant serves predictable foods at reasonable prices.

Open all year ❖ Credit cards: Visa/CB, Eurocard/Access, American Express ❖ Rooms: double 350 F, breakfast 35 F ❖ Menus: 63 F, 83 F, menu enfant 39 F ❖ à la carte: about 100 F ❖ Parking ❖ English spoken

---

RESTAURANT

L'Huîtrière

3, rue des Chats-Bossus
tel.: 20 55 43 41
fax: 20 55 23 10

The tiled front of this long-standing, Lillois institution, located in the heart of atmospheric Vieux Lille, opens on to banks of the freshest shellfish and fish and, past the *poissonnerie*, leads to the warm, classic and elegant dining room of a traditional restaurant that is widely rated as one of the city's best. Of course, you can simply soak in the surroundings while enjoying *huîtres* by the dozen here as well as superlative *plateaux de fruits de mer* but the cuisine of chef François Fouassier is much more considered than this: dishes which stand out include *huîtres chaudes au Champagne, galette de pommes de terre à l'anguille fumée et aux poireaux, lasagne de langouste rouge et de pointes d'asperges, homard aux*

légumes façon waterzooï and, for carnivores, superlative *agneau de lait de Pauillac.* An extensive and exceptional wine list plus creative desserts round off a great, gastronomic experience.

Closed Sun. evening and Aug. ❖ Credit cards: Visa/CB, Eurocard/Access, American Express, Diners ❖ Menus: 350 F, 450 F, 500 F ❖ à la carte: about 450 F ❖ English spoken

L'Huîtrière, Lille

RESTAURANT

La Coquille
60, rue de St-Etienne
tel.: 20 54 29 82

This typical Vieux Lille restaurant, located in a well-restored house centrally located by the Palais de Congrès, has a warm and intimate atmosphere and is noted, above all, for Olivier Deleval's light, modern cuisine which makes good use of regional ingredients. He likes to use the local *bière de garde* in cooking as in *le râble de lapereau rôti à la bière caramélisé* and seeks his poultry from Licques and fish and shellfish from Boulogne. Olivier lived and worked in the United States for five years before returning to his home and he speaks perfect English.

Closed Sat. midday, Sun., three weeks in Aug., one week in Feb. ❖ Credit card: Visa/CB ❖ Menus: 130 F, 150 F (all inclusive, midday only), 168 F, 235 F ❖ à la carte: about 200 F ❖ English spoken

---

BRASSERIE

**Brasserie
Lutterbach**
10, rue Faidherbe
tel.: 20 55 13 74

Lille is a city whose inhabitants like to eat well and heartily, and throughout this major metropolis there are scores of good, everyday restaurants and *brasseries* which fit the bill very well and satisfy the cavernous appetites of local business-men, workers and visitors alike. The Lutterbach, centrally located opposite the old Bourse just off the Grande Place, is a case in point, a stylish but classic eating house serving hearty *brasserie*-style foods rapidly, professionally and with some good humour. Typical dishes here include *tarte au Maroilles, choucroute, le confit de canard à la crème de ciboulette* and good grilled meats and fish. There is always a *plat du jour* and a good selection of both inexpensive wines and beers.

Closed first fortnight in Aug. ❖ Credit cards: Visa/CB, Eurocard/Access, American Express, Diners ❖ Menus: 80 F, 105 F, 120 F, menu enfant 55 F ❖ à la carte: about 150 F

RESTAURANT-
FROMAGERIE

Christian Leclerq
9-11, rue Lepelletier
tel.: 20 74 17 05

Christian Leclerq is passionate about cheese: his shop-cum-restaurant located in Vieux Lille is the place to visit if you share his enthusiasm. For us, we must confess, that a meal entirely centred around *les fromages de France* can be a little hard to stomach, but for lovers of cheese *tartes, fondue, raclette* and the like, this is definitely the place to come. Alternatively, after a walking tour of Vieux Lille, why not pop in for a *grande dégustation* of cheeses from throughout the country, accompanied by a good bottle of red wine.

Closed Sun., Mon. and Aug. ❖ Credit cards: Visa/CB, Eurocard/Access ❖ à la carte: about 100–150 F

Vieux Lille

62990 LOISON-SUR-CRÉQUOISE (PAS DE CALAIS) 🍴

Festivals   *Fête de la Groseille*   Sun. after 14 July
            Fête du Cidre   third weekend in Oct.
Calais 75 km – Le Touquet 30 km – Hesdin 14 km

CRÊPERIE EN PLEIN AIR

La Maison du Perlé
50, rue Principale
tel.: 21 81 30 85
fax: 21 86 05 80

Hubert Delobel's *crêperie en plein air* is little more than a hut set amidst the gardens and playground of the Maison du Perlé where he manufactures his now locally famous sparkling fruit wines. But it is worth mentioning for outstanding *crêpes*, made with beer to give them extra lightness, filled with cheese, ham and *crème fraîche*, followed by sweet versions made with a fresh *coulis de framboise*. This is a simple, light repast but one to enjoy with a *flûte* of *Perlé de Groseille* (made with redcurrants) or *Perlé de Framboise* (drier, made with raspberries) or with a glass of local cider or apple juice.

Afterwards, so fortified, take a walk or rent a mountain bike for an excursion through the beautiful Vallée de la Créquoise.

Open Sun. only June and Sept., daily July and Aug. (in good weather) ❖ Credit cards: Visa/CB, Eurocard/Access, American Express ❖ Menus: 40 F, 60 F ❖ English spoken

---

62380 LUMBRES (PAS DE CALAIS)
Calais 42 km – Boulogne-sur-Mer 39 km – St-Omer 10 km

HOTEL-RESTAURANT

Auberge de Moulin de Mombreux
route de Bayenghem
tel.: 21 39 13 13
　　　21 39 62 44
fax: 21 93 61 34

The seventeenth-century, stone millhouse poised suggestively over the tiny River Blécquin is indeed a beautiful setting for the lovely restaurant owned by Jean-Marc and Danielle Gaudry, considered to be one of the best in the region. Come here to enjoy Jean-Marc's light and precise cuisine, noted, above all, for its imaginative use of the freshest produce and products from the surrounding area – seafood and shellfish from Boulogne, fresh vegetables and market produce from the *marais audomarois*, poultry from Licques. On a recent visit, specialities included *soupe de moules aux pommes de terre et chou-fleur, pâté de canard en croûte, turbot rôti à la bière, suprême de volaille de Licques crème d'ail* and a feather-light *soufflé à l'anis*.

Moulin de Mombreux, Lumbres

There are twenty-three bedrooms in a newly constructed annexe. They are rated 4-star but quite frankly, though well equipped, furnished traditionally, with French windows that open on to either the mill or the countryside, they are not overly spacious or luxurious. Seven rooms each have an extra pull-out sofa; however, if this is utilized, then a supplement of 30% is added to the room rate. We can only assume that this is a means of discouraging couples with children.

Closed 20–28 Dec. ❖ Credit cards: Visa/CB, Eurocard/Access, American Express, Diners ❖ Menus: 180 F, 300 F, 400 F ❖ à la carte: about 400 F ❖ Rooms: double 580–650 F (30% supplement for extra bed), breakfast 56 F ❖ Parking ❖ English spoken

---

59550 MAROILLES (NORD) 🛒

Marché Thur.
Festival *Fête de la Flamiche* Sun. before 15 Aug.
Calais 192 km – Cambrai 42 km – Avesnes-sur-Helpe 14 km

CAFÉ-RESTAURANT

Café-Restaurant de Ferme du Verger Pilote
1810, route de Landrecies
tel.: 27 84 71 10
fax: 27 77 77 23

Located just outside Maroilles, this large, modern café looks little different from any other roadside inn. However, this is a genuine farmhouse restaurant attached to the village's

Tartes aux fruits, Maroilles

only remaining producer of farmhouse cheese, the Ferme du Verger Pilote. Come here to sample the great Maroilles cheese at the source and other simple foods such as *assiette campagnarde*, *flamiche au Maroilles*, *andouillette de Cambrai* accompanied by a glass of local Jenlain beer or a bottle of farmhouse cider. Afterwards, purchase cheese and other regional products in the adjoining shop.

Café-Restaurant open daily. Full meals midday only. Guided visits to the cheese dairy and ageing *caves* Sun. and holidays 1600–1800 or by appointment ❖ Credit cards: Visa/CB, Eurocard/Access ❖ Menus: 55 F, 60 F, 90 F ❖ à la carte: about 100 F

62170 MONTREUIL-SUR-MER (PAS DE CALAIS) 🛒

Marché   Sat.
Calais 70 km – Boulogne-sur-Mer 37 km – Abbeville 42 km

HOTEL-RESTAURANT

Les Hauts de Montreuil

21–23, rue Pierre Ledent
tel.: 21 81 95 92
fax: 21 86 28 83

Les Hauts de Montreuil is an ancient *hôtellerie* located in the fortified heart of old Montreuil in what is claimed to be the town's oldest building, a classified *monument historique* dating from 1537. Today, it is a hotel with a highly rated gastronomic restaurant, wine bar and wine and cheese *cave*, run personally and passionately by its exuberant and ebullient owner, Monsieur Jacques Gantiez. At present, the bedrooms are all located in a newly built annexe to the rear of the original building off the central courtyard. Somewhat motel-like in character, each is, nonetheless, modern, immaculate and well equipped with private bathroom and w.c., television, telephone, mini-bar and hair dryer. At the time of writing, additional bedrooms and two more suites are in the process of being renovated in an adjacent, period building.

The dining rooms are located on the ground and first floors of the atmospheric, beamed, old inn. In this historic setting, classic cuisine with a strong, regional accent is served in a range of good menus which change with the seasons. The selection of local and regional cheeses, turned, brushed, washed and aged to maturity by Monsieur Gantiez himself in the *cave à fromages* in the vaulted cellars below the restaurant, is superb. The wine list must rank as one of the finest in the region, strong on classics but with a good selection of inexpensive and medium-priced wines, too. Some twenty-two different wines are available by the glass (again, ranging from house wine to classed growth clarets) so it is quite feasible to enjoy a different wine with each course. There is even a connoisseur's *carte des cafés* offered after the meal with a selection of fine coffees together with detailed tasting notes.

Wines by the glass and simple cold snacks and light meals (plates of local cheese, air-dried *saucisson* and other meats) are served in the bar.

Closed Mon., and Jan. ❖ Credit cards: Visa/CB, Eurocard/Access ❖ Rooms: double 350–380 F, buffet breakfast 40 F ❖ Menus: 120 F, 160 F, 210 F ❖ à la carte: about 240 F ❖ Parking ❖ English spoken ❖ L S H B

Les Hauts de Montreuil, Montreuil-sur-Mer

HOTEL

Hôtel de France
2, rue Petit Coquempot
tel.: 21 06 05 36

This is one of the most curious and individual hotels that we have encountered. An original, seventeenth-century *relais* located in the heart of old Montreuil opposite the ninth-century town ramparts, it has literally been receiving guests and travellers for nearly 400 years: kings of both France and England are reputed to have stopped here en route between Paris and Calais, while Victor Hugo based an episode in *Les Misérables* in the hotel and Laurence Sterne wrote much of *A Sentimental Journey through France and Italy* while staying here. During the First World War, British Commander-in-Chief Field-Marshal Douglas Haig lived in

Hôtel de France,
Montreuil-sur-Mer

the hotel. Today, it is a small, historic character hotel with fifteen bedrooms (eleven with private bath and w.c.), owned by Janie Hall and Phil Spear-Bailey who are both English.

Haphazard, even a little chaotic, though the hotel undoubtedly is, this is, nonetheless, a professional and well-run operation full of charm, character and English wit. It is not, however, the place to come to if you are looking for sanitized, standardized rooms with modern fittings, furnishings, plumbing and English television (there is no television at all). Come here, instead, to stay in an ancient, historic coaching inn that is part of the very fabric of Montreuil's history, decorated personally, even idiosyncratically, and with considerable style and panache.

Open all year ❖ Credit cards: Visa/CB, Eurocard/Access ❖ Rooms: double 330 F, breakfast 40 F ❖ Parking ❖ English and some Italian spoken

Small Hotels and Restaurants

RESTAURANT
WITH ROOMS

**Hôtel-Restaurant
Le Darnétal**
place Darnétal
tel.: 21 06 04 87

This centrally located, highly regarded, small restaurant with a few rooms is owned and run by Lisa and Jean-Paul Vernay. Jean-Paul, who is the chef, is a Burgundian, trained in classic French traditions, and the cuisine here reflects this: house specialities include *huîtres tièdes au Champagne, nage de St-Jacques aux légumes, foie gras de canard, saumon beurre blanc, turbot poché sauce hollandaise, confit de canard*. The dining room is rather intimate and atmospheric and the welcome is genuine.

There are four rooms available, fairly basic and simply furnished, each with private shower or bath and w.c.

Restaurant closed Mon. evening, Tue. ❖ Credit cards: Visa/CB, Eurocard/Access, American Express, Diners ❖ Menus: 90 F (weekdays only), 130 F, 165 F, 180 F ❖ à la carte: about 200 F ❖ Rooms: double 230–260 F

RESTAURANT
WITH ROOMS

*3 km W. at
Madeleine-sous-
Montreuil*

**Auberge de la
Grenouillère**
tel.: 21 06 07 22
fax: 21 86 36 36

The Auberge de la Grenouillère is certainly one of the most appealing and idyllic small inns in the north of France, combining at the same time a natural, country atmosphere with great style, finesse and cooking of the highest order. Roland and Claudine Gauthier are charming and warm and make their guests feel immediately welcome and relaxed. In good weather, meals are served outdoors in the lovely, flowered courtyard in front of the *auberge* which overlooks the Canche while at other times guests dine in the low, atmospheric, beamed rooms of the inn, the most famous of which is decorated with charming frescos that illustrate a fable by La Fontaine in which an impeccably dressed frog eats and eats until he explodes.

Roland Gauthier's cuisine is flavoursome, precise and, above all, exceedingly fresh, utilizing the finest local produce from the sea and country alike, perfumed extensively with fresh herbs grown in the *potager* behind the inn. Naturally, the menus and *carte* change with the seasons but there is always a *menu du terroir* and a *menu de la mer*. Dishes which stand out include *langoustines grillées aux arômes de genièvre et orange confite, nage d'huîtres de pleine mer au parfum de crustacé et orge perlé, suprême de bar rôti sur le peau* and *carré d'agneau de pré-salé de la Baie de la Somme*. These are foods that really taste good, beautifully presented certainly but not over fussily, and are eminently satisfying and delicious. Cheeses come from Philippe Olivier and desserts are light and beautiful.

The Grenouillère has four comfortable rooms, all arranged around the courtyard, furnished brightly and with well-appointed private facilities. While two rooms are small, there is also a larger room and a suite.

Closed Tue. evening, Wed. (except July–Aug.), 15 Dec.–15 Jan. ❖Credit cards: Visa/CB, Eurocard/Access, American Express, Diners ❖ Menus: 130 F (weekdays only), 190 F, 250 F, 330 F ❖ à la carte: about 350 F ❖ Rooms: double 300–400 F, suite 500 F, breakfast 40 F ❖ Some English spoken

Roland Gauthier,
Auberge de la Grenouillère,
Madeleine-sous-Montreuil

62890 RECQUES-SUR-HEM (PAS DE CALAIS)

Calais 16 km – Ardres 9 km – St-Omer 18 km

HOTEL-RESTAURANT-WINE SHOP

Château de Cocove
tel.: 21 82 68 29
fax: 21 82 72 59

It is hard to believe that this excellent château hotel is so close to Calais and England: at once atmospheric and grand, it is at the same time wholly welcoming, intimate and relaxing. The château was constructed in the eighteenth century and was completely restored in 1986 by the present owners. The bedrooms overlook the front park which is part of the 11-hectare grounds of the estate. This is isolated, quiet, rural France *par excellence*, a perfect idyll only slightly jarred by the fact that nearly all the guests at Cocove are likely to be British. No matter: for while catering almost exclusively for us, Cocove, with its young, mainly female staff who all speak excellent English, at the same time manages to maintain an atmosphere that is wholly and genuinely *très français*.

There are twenty-three bedrooms in this 3-star hotel, the majority of which overlook the impressive front park. All are comfortably decorated and each has private bath, w.c., satellite television and telephone. The largest rooms, which are a little more expensive, are grand indeed. The restaurant, in a rather austere dining room with stone walls and large glass windows which overlook the park, serves classic foods with a regional accent. The 160 F menu, for example, offers *salade au confit de lapereau* or *coquilles St-Jacques à l'huile de noix*, then *volaille de Licques forestière* or *lotte au confit d'échalote*, followed by a good selection of mainly regional *fromages*, and a rich *crème brulée* to finish. Cocove, however, might well be a restaurant where you would prefer to choose your wines before deciding what to eat: the wine list is comprehensive and superb and prices are reasonable.

The owner of the hotel, Monsieur Didier Calonne, is a

Château de Cocove, Recques-sur-Hem

long-established, local wine *négociant* who bought the château as something of a hobby rather than a principle activity. Nonetheless, he has found that it has proved to be an excellent outlet for his range of wines offered not just in the restaurant but by the glass or bottle at the bar and also for sale in the 'Wine Shop' located in the château cellars. This indeed provides a serious opportunity for purchasing good wines at fair prices.

Closed 24–25 Dec. ❖Credit cards: Visa/CB, Eurocard/Access, American Express, Diners ❖ Rooms: double 415 F, 475 F, 660 F, breakfast 40 F ❖ Menus: 70 F, 105 F, 160 F, 205 F ❖ à la carte: about 250 F ❖ Parking ❖ English and German spoken ❖ L S H B

62500 ST-OMER (PAS DE CALAIS) 🛒
Marché Wed., Sat.
Calais 46 km – Boulogne-sur-Mer 49 km – Lille 67 km

HOTEL-RESTAURANT

Le Bretagne

2, place du Vainquai
tel.: 21 38 25 78
fax: 21 93 51 22

The Bretagne has long been rated as probably St-Omer's best hotel, well situated near the l'Aa waterfront and the ruins of St-Bertrain, within easy walking distance of the town centre. The seventy-six 3-star rooms are comfortable if somewhat characterless: all have private facilities (either bath or shower, and w.c.), television and telephone.

The Bretagne is a good choice if you wish to eat in your hotel. There are three separate restaurants which cater for different tastes and occasions. Le Best is a *restaurant gastronomique* which has a high reputation locally; Le Petit Best is more accessible with an easy, family style and a popular formula that includes choice of entrée and main course; and the Grill Maeva offers both good value menus as well as simple entrées and grills.

Credit cards: Visa/CB, Eurocard/Access, American Express, Diners ❖ Rooms: double 400 F, breakfast 50 F ❖ Menus: 90 F, 165 F, 185 F (including wine) ❖ à la carte: about 150–300 F ❖ Parking ❖ English spoken

Small Hotels and Restaurants

HOTEL-RESTAURANT

**Hôtel-Restaurant
St-Louis**

25, rue d'Arras

tel.: 21 38 35 21

fax: 21 38 57 26

The St-Louis is a pleasant and friendly, 2-star *Logis de France* located in the centre of this popular market town. Most of the thirty simply furnished, modernish rooms have private facilities (bath or shower, and w.c.), television and telephone; quieter, if somewhat darker rooms are located in an annexe behind the hotel. The lively bar is open all day and is a popular meeting place for the town's youth.

The Restaurant Flaubert is a favourite with locals and serves traditional and regional foods: *flamiche aux poireaux, salade aux foies de volaille, coquilles St-Jacques, choucroute, carbonnade à la flamande, jambonneau au poivre vert*. The menus are good value.

Open all year ❖ Credit cards: Visa/CB, Eurocard/Access ❖ Rooms: double 285 F, breakfast 29 F ❖ Menus: 66 F, 88 F, 140 F, menu enfant 50 F ❖ à la carte: about 150 F ❖ Parking ❖ English and German spoken ❖ L S H B

RESTAURANT

Le Cygne

8, rue Caventou

tel.: 21 98 20 52

St-Omer is a smart, little town and we like it very much simply as a place to come for shopping, for an overnight stop en route to or from Calais or just to wander around the old *centre ville* which has a remarkable and well-preserved number of seventeenth- and eighteenth-century, merchants' houses. Le Cygne is located in one such typical house on a quiet square just a few minutes' walk from the Grande Place. There are two dining rooms: the one on the ground floor is furnished smartly and traditionally; the one in the

vaulted cellar is more atmospheric. This is a satisfying and classic, *bourgeois* restaurant, appreciated locally for its well-prepared and generous menus. Chef Jean-François Wident utilizes wherever possible the good, local produce and products of the *audomarois*, and specialities include *foie gras maison*, duck

Le Cygne, St-Omer

in a variety of ways (*magret de canard aux girolles, magret de canard aux cerises*), *coquelet au genièvre de Houlle, la gainée boulonnaise, escalope de turbot.*

Closed Mon. evening, Tue., and two weeks in Feb. ❖ Credit cards: Visa/CB, Eurocard/Access ❖ Menus: 72 F (weekdays only), 90 F, 135 F, 180 F ❖ à la carte: about 250 F

CHAMBRE D'HÔTE AND *TABLE D'HÔTE*

3 km N.E. at Clairmarais

Marie-Laure Galamez

2, route du Grande Nieppe

tel.: 21 93 25 41

The *marais audomarois*, located virtually on the edge of St-Omer, is an area of rare, unspoiled beauty that must be visited. Clairmarais is the centre for walks and excursions by boat into this unique and secret wetland of marshes crisscrossed by canals.

Marie-Laure and Claude Galamez have a lovely smallholding on the edge of the *marais* where they offer *chambres*. When we arrived at this charming, virtually self-sufficient farm, the couple were in the process of slaughtering a pig with the help of an itinerant *charcutier*. Don't let this put you off, though: this is a once a year event and afterwards, everyone pitched in to help salt the hams and to make the sausages and *boudin*. Claude is a local general practitioner, Marie-Laure a talented artist: their lives, though, are governed by the seasons in this lovely and idylic, rural smallholding. Here they grow vegetables, fruit and flowers

Marais audomarois near St-Omer

in their garden, raise sheep and chickens, keep bees, and fish for eels and smallfry in their lake and in the canals.

The Galamezs offer two new *chambres*, each with private shower and shared w.c., located above the newly built garage next to the farmhouse. If given sufficient notice, Marie-Laure will provide *table d'hôte* meals. She is an excellent cook and utilizes almost exclusively her own fresh produce.

Rooms: two persons 160 F, three persons 210 F including breakfast ❖ Table d'hôte: about 60–80 F per person ❖ A little English spoken

---

RESTAURANT

3 km N.E. at Clairmarais

Auberge des Nénuphars
60, route de St-Omer
tel.: 21 38 24 84

Come out to the *marais audomarois* to purchase vegetables from the small growers who cultivate the rich, alluvial lands of the marshes, to take a boat trip in a distinctive, wooden, traditional *bacove* and to eat at this extremely friendly and excellent restaurant. Madame Dumont, the proprietor, prepares local foods (*anguilles* from the canals in a variety of ways), good seafood (*brioche de crabe*), and hearty home-cooked dishes (*paupiettes de volaille aux girolles, tête de veau sauce gribiche*) followed by sensational fruit tarts usually served straight from the oven. In summer, meals can be enjoyed outside in the garden beside the canal.

Credit cards: Visa/CB, Eurocard/Access ❖ Menus: 60 F, 90 F, 130 F ❖ à la carte: about 150 F

HOTEL-RESTAURANT

5 km N.W. at Tilques

Hôtel-Restaurant Château Tilques
off N43
tel.: 21 93 28 99
fax: 21 38 34 23
Reservations European Country Hotels
tel.: (081) 940 2317

The Château Tilques, a nineteenth-century, neo-Flemish mansion set within its own 10-hectare park, is an English-owned, 4-star château hotel-restaurant. There are fifty-two rooms, twenty-eight of which are located in the main château itself, twenty-four in a new, purpose-built, adjoining annexe. While the main, ground-floor reception of the hotel, the lovely period *salon* and bar, and the conservatory breakfast room are atmospheric and beautifully furnished as befits a grand château hotel, the bedrooms in the château itself, though they all have private facilities and enjoy pleasant views over the grounds, are not yet up to the level of the rest of the establishment. The rooms in the new annexe, on the other hand, are spacious, modern and extremely comfortable with large bathrooms and terraces overlooking the park. But, and here's the rub, being modern they lack period character and they are considerably more expensive than those in the château.

No criticism, however, can be levelled at the restaurant which must be one of the best in the region and certainly a reason in itself for a visit here. The dining room is located in the atmospheric, converted stables of the château, a long, formal room with pleasant, candle-lit tables. Patrick Hittos is a talented chef and serves traditional foods based on fine, regional produce, prepared and presented with skill and finesse. His *menu du marché* changes regularly according to what is available and in season. Dishes we particularly enjoyed included *sauté de cuisses de grenouilles à l'ail nouveau*, *galette de thon aux pistils de safran* and *fricassée de lotte au vin liqueureux*. Local cheeses are served with home-baked breads, and desserts are light and delicious.

Breakfast is served either in the rooms or in the garden conservatory. There is a tennis court and a putting green while boat or mountain bike excursions can be arranged to explore the *marais audomarois*.

Open all year ❖ Credit cards: Visa/ CB, Eurocard/Access, American Express, Diners ❖ Rooms: double in château 480–580 F, double in new annexe 750 F, breakfast 50 F ❖ Menus: lunch 125 F and 145 F, dinner 165 F and 195 F, menu enfant 40 F ❖ à la carte: about 350 F ❖ Parking ❖ English, German, Spanish and Arabic spoken

Château Tilques, Tilques

Small Hotels and Restaurants

HOTEL-RESTAURANT

5 km S.W. at
Wisques

Hôtel-Restaurant
La Sapinière
tel.: 21 95 14 59
fax: 21 93 28 72

La Sapinière,
Wisques

When we dropped in on Henri-Michel Delbèke he was looking after his children as his wife Anne-Marie had just given birth to a new baby only a few weeks earlier. Their comfortable, 2-star *Logis de France* conveniently located just outside St-Omer near the A26 *autoroute* is definitely a place where families will feel welcome. In addition to the fifteen rooms in the 200-year-old country house, most having their own private bath, shower and w.c., television and telephone, the couple are in the process of completing three new annexes of six rooms each, all with full private facilities. Each chalet will have a large family room that can sleep five or six.

The comfortable, airy dining room overlooking the rolling *audomarois* countryside, is noted for its authentic and carefully prepared, regional cooking. Each menu offers local dishes including *flamiche aux poireaux du marais, carbonnade à la flamande, coq à la bière des Trois Monts, blanquette d'escargots d'Artois mode de l'Abbaye, homard à la bière.* 'Our cuisine is strictly traditional,' says Monsieur Delbèke. 'We use plenty of butter and cream: perhaps not so good for

la ligne,' he added, patting his stomach. *'Mais très bon pour le goût.'*

Open all year. Restaurant closed Sun. evening, Mon. midday ❖ Credit cards: Visa/CB, Eurocard/Access, American Express ❖ Rooms: double 220–300 F, breakfast 25 F ❖ Menus: 60 F, 95 F, 130 F, 160 F, 200 F, menu enfant 40 F ❖ à la carte: about 150 F ❖ Parking ❖ A little English spoken

---

59190 STAPLE (NORD)
Calais 56 km – Hazebrouck 7 km – St-Omer 12 km

FERME AUBERGE

La Rabaude

190, rue du Berger

tel.: 28 40 03 28

La Rabaude, Staple

The Lachèvre family raise free-range poultry, rabbits, pigs, cows and grow vegetables on their farm on the rich, fertile plain of Flanders. They utilize their own produce and products in the rustic dining room of their welcoming *ferme auberge*. Madame Lachèvre, assisted by her mother, prepares typical foods of the Nord: *flamiche aux poireaux, flamiche au Maroilles, lapin aux pruneaux, coq à la bière, pintade aux poires*. There is always a good selection of local cheeses

and homemade desserts on offer. The *ferme auberge* is extremely popular with people from Hazebrouck, Lille and Belgium, so it is essential to reserve.

There are two very simple and basic *chambres* available, each with a double bed, as well as a pleasant campsite.

Open all year Sat. evening, Sun. midday by reservation; daily July–Aug. by reservation; out of season by reservation for groups. ❖ Menus: 90–120 F ❖ Rooms: two persons 125 F including breakfast ❖ Some English spoken

---

62520 LE TOUQUET (PAS DE CALAIS) 🐎

Marché   Thur., Sat.; Mon. in season
Calais 63 km – Boulogne-sur-Mer 31 km

HOTEL

Hôtel Red Fox
angle rue St-Jean-rue de Metz
tel.: 21 05 27 58
fax: 21 05 27 56

The biggest plus for this friendly, modern, 2-star hotel is its location in the heart of Le Touquet on its main drag just a five-minute walk from the seafront; the biggest drawback is its location in the heart of town where all the action is, where the young people from the town and round about come in search of nightclubs and drink and generally have a good, fairly harmless but noisy time. When staying in Le Touquet, you must decide whether you want to be central where it is lively or further out where it is quiet but a long way from town.

If you want the former, then the Red Fox is definitely the place to stay. The forty-eight rooms here may not have any character but they are clean, modern and have excellent private facilities, satellite television and telephones; also they seem to be reasonably sound-proofed. In addition to the normal, fairly small doubles, there are about a dozen larger rooms which would be suitable for families. There is no restaurant but there are plenty on the doorstep including Serge Pérard just a few doors away. There is also a private garage for parking located 100 metres away.

Open all year ❖ Credit cards: Visa/CB, Eurocard/Access ❖ Rooms: double 420–510 F, buffet breakfast 40 F ❖ Parking ❖ English spoken ❖ L S H B

CHAMBRE D'HÔTE

Le Polo

allée des Pâquerettes
tel.: 21 05 18 14

Madame Lucie Bournoville offers four pleasant *chambres* in her family house located in the *fôret de Touquet*, the peaceful, wooded, residental area that lies on the outskirts of Le Touquet, far from the madness and bustle of the town centre. The rooms are lovely and bright and overlook the beautiful, flowered garden. Though the rooms do not have their own private facilities, Madame ensures that everything is kept spotlessly clean. Now that her own children have grown up, she has begun to offer the *chambres* to visitors as a hobby and for the chance to meet people. She is warm, welcoming and genuine. Her home makes a pleasant, welcome alternative to staying in the town centre or in the expensive, luxury hotels just outside.

Open all year ❖ Rooms: two persons 220 F including breakfast

RESTAURANT

Le Café des Arts

80, rue de Paris
tel.: 21 05 21 55

This stylish, deceptively simple-looking restaurant just up from the seafront, decorated rather minimally with contemporary paintings, is rated by many locals to be the best in town. The cuisine reflects the decor and ambiance, strictly modern, inventive, original and of the highest order, presented stylishly, even artistically, in a refined atmosphere which is at great odds with the general hullaballoo of Le Touquet in full cry during the season. Come here to sample the *menu tentation* which is put together freshly each day according to what chef Jérôme Panni finds at market, based, of course, primarily on exceptionally fresh shellfish and fish.

Closed Mon.; Tue. except in July and Aug. ❖ Credit cards: Visa/CB, Eurocard/Access, American Express, Diners ❖ Menus: 140 F, 300 F ❖ à la carte: about 350 F ❖ English spoken

RESTAURANT

Serge Pérard

67, rue de Metz
tel.: 21 05 13 33
fax: 21 05 62 32

Serge Pérard is famous, above all, for his fish soup, made daily in immense cauldrons in the adjoining *poissonnerie*, served fresh in the restaurant (as much as you can eat), or else sold bottled to be carried away by the crate by Parisians and English alike as well as shipped around the world.

Serge Pérard,
Le Touquet

The restaurant, with its pavement tables on Le Touquet's main drag, and large, informal dining room, is really quite fun. Indeed, a visit here is a must to enjoy basically simple foods – *soupe de poissons* (of course) as well as a new, excellent *soupe de crabes*, platters of *fruits de mer* and impeccably fresh fish, best simply fried or grilled. Afterwards, repair next door to purchase your obligatory jars of the famous soup to take back home with you.

Open daily ❖ No credit cards ❖ Menus: 95 F, 138 F ❖ à la carte: about 150–200 F ❖ English spoken

---

62142 LE WAST (PAS DE CALAIS)
Calais 30 km – Boulogne 15 km – St-Omer 35 km

HOTEL-RESTAURANT

Hostellerie du Château des Tourelles
tel.: 21 33 34 78
fax: 21 87 59 57

This country hotel, in spite of its name, is not a grand château but a simple, 2-star, family-run *Logis de France*. There are eighteen bedrooms located in the eighteenth-century country house, clean, serviceable, even somewhat characterful in a certain French provincial way; all the rooms have their own private bath or shower, w.c., and telephone. The annexe has some adjoining rooms with shared bathroom which would be suitable for families.

We like it here: this is a friendly place to come with

friends or family, to relax in the quiet country, explore the many footpaths of the *espace naturel régional* of Le Wast, play tennis or table tennis, or to use as a base for shopping excursions. In the evenings, relax in the hotel's restaurant where owner Serge Feutry serves superior, traditional cuisine, particularly utilizing fresh fish from Boulogne. Specialities of the house include own-smoked salmon, *escalope de saumon à la crème d'oseille, filet de turbot aux girolles*, and, for meat-eaters, *mignon de bœuf aux morilles* and the local favourite *coq à la bière*. Absolutely everything here is *fait maison* including all the desserts and *pâtisseries*. There is an excellent wine list which includes some old vintages in good condition.

Closed two weeks in Feb. ❖ Credit cards: Visa/CB, Eurocard/Access, American Express ❖ Rooms: double 240 F, breakfast 25 F ❖ Menus: 80 F, 120 F, 150 F, 200 F ❖ à la carte: about 200 F ❖ English spoken

---

62720 WIERRE-EFFROY (PAS DE CALAIS) 🛒

Calais 30 km – Boulogne-sur-Mer 12 km – Marquise 5 km

HOTEL-RESTAURANT

Ferme du Vert

tel.: 21 87 67 00
fax: 21 83 22 62

The Ferme du Vert is one of the most delightful and idyllic farmhouse hotels that we have encountered, still a real, working farm which has been transformed into a comfortable and professional, 3-star *Logis de France* by the Bernard family.

Ferme du Vert,
Wierre-Effroy

There are fifteen rooms located in the original farmhouse and surrounding outbuildings which are arranged around the central *cœur*. Though they are classified as 3-star, don't come here expecting standards equivalent to those in a city centre establishment. The rooms, though full of character with wood panelling, beams, old, rustic furniture, are basically still farmhouse accommodation, albeit comfortably so with central heating and private bathrooms (eleven with showers, four with baths), w.c. and direct dial telephone. This is a place to come to enjoy a beautiful and idyllic, rural setting in the lovely Boulonnais countryside, a warm and genuine family welcome, good country foods and, an added bonus, their own outstanding farmhouse cheeses.

Son Thomas is the chef in the restaurant Le Petit Patre and he produces cuisine that is a considerable notch above many farmhouse restaurants that we have encountered. There is always a choice of *entrées*, then a *plat du jour*, a selection of cheeses from the farm and a selection of desserts. The vegetable soup served in a tureen is always a warming and welcome start to a meal, and on a recent visit we enjoyed *filet mignon de porc à la moutarde et vinaigre de framboise*. Son Antoine, an artisan *fromager*, supplies an outstanding range of farmhouse cheeses all made on the premises.

There are mountain bikes which you can hire by the day as well as a putting green (though you may have to dodge ducks and geese).

Open all year ❖ Credit cards: Visa/CB, Eurocard/Access ❖ Rooms: double 350–490 F, breakfast 42 F ❖ Menus: 130 F, menu enfant 60 F ❖ English spoken

---

62930 WIMEREUX (PAS DE CALAIS) 🚂

Festival   *Fête de la Moule*   first Sun. in Aug.
Calais 29 km – Boulogne-sur-Mer 5 km

HOTEL-RESTAURANT

Hôtel Atlantic
Digue de Mer
tel.: 21 32 41 01
fax: 21 87 46 17

The Atlantic is a notable landmark on this stretch of coast. Aron and Marie-France Misan who formerly owned the Keats Restaurant in Hampstead, took over in 1990 and totally refurbished the hotel as well as redecorated the striking, first-floor dining room which overlooks the sea. There are eleven bedrooms, six of which enjoy superb sea views – on a good day you can see across to England.

All of the rooms, while not overly spacious, are brightly decorated, well-equipped and comfortable, each with private bath or shower, w.c., television and telephone.

Most importantly, the airy, open restaurant located on the first floor has been restored to something like its former glory. Chef Alain Morville is talented and creative, and makes full use of the superlative seafood and shellfish available from France's number one fishing port, Boulogne. Downstairs, there is a bar-*brasserie* serving simple but good, local foods – *soupe de poissons*, *moules marinières*, a plate of smoked salmon with *pain aux algues* (seaweed bread) – indoors out of season, on the seafront terrace in summer, from where you watch the windsurfers dodge the Seacat.

Closed Sun. evening, Mon. except in July and Aug., 1 Dec.–1 March ❖ Credit cards: Visa/CB, Eurocard/Access ❖ Rooms: double 350–420 F, breakfast 40 F ❖ Menus: 110 F, 190 F ❖ à la carte: about 300 F ❖ English, Italian and Spanish spoken

62179 WISSANT (PAS DE CALAIS)
Calais 18 km – Boulogne-sur-Mer 18 km

HOTEL-RESTAURANT

Hôtel de la Plage

place Edouard Houssin
tel.: (Hôtel) 21 35 91 87
(Restaurant) 21 82 78 32
fax: 21 85 48 10

This somewhat dated (even, dare we say, a little shabby) hotel dates from 1888 and is reminiscent of something of the *début de siècle* grandeur which the small seaside resorts between Calais and Boulogne once enjoyed. Today, as then, this quiet, old fishing town with a long, sandy beach is patronized by foreigners more than the French, mainly the Belgians, English and Dutch.

The Plage is a real old-style French hotel that seems from another age. The forty-five rooms in the old part of the hotel are extremely basic, small, rather dismal but five new rooms, all nonsmoking, have been built in an adjoining, modern annexe which, though lacking the character of the old building, are well equipped, each with private bathroom, w.c., television and telephone; a few are large enough to accommodate a family. If one of these new rooms is available, then the Plage could make an ideal weekend hideaway.

The traditional, rather old-fashioned, family-style ambiance is also evident in the restaurant. The characterful,

*Hôtel de la Plage,
Wissant*

old *salle à manger* is really *vieille française* and here you can enjoy mainly traditional foods based on the excellent seafood and shellfish of the area – *la coquille de fruits de mer gratinée, brochette de poissons, sole meunière*. The menus are good value and there is an excellent wine cellar with some good, aged clarets at reasonable prices.

Open all year ❖ Rooms: double in the old part 148–170 F, double in the new annexe 265–320 F, breakfast 35 F ❖ Menus: 80 F, 100 F, 120 F ❖ à la carte: about 150 F ❖ English and Dutch spoken

PICARDY

Picardy, the link between Calais, Paris and the rest of France, has often served as a region to travel through, rather than stop in, probably since the days of the Romans. This should finally be set to change, and for good reason. Picardy is quite simply one of the most beautiful, gentle and welcoming parts of northern France. Moreover, it is quite literally on the doorstep of the Channel Tunnel and it has more than enough to offer in terms of scenery, history, architecture and good, small hotels and restaurants for the visitor crossing over for a short break.

Amiens, the capital of the region, is certainly one of the great cities of northern France. It deserves to be visited for its great, Gothic cathedral, claimed to be the largest in Christendom,

Senlis cathedral

as well as for its atmospheric *hortillonages*, a vast and extensive area of reclaimed marshland crisscrossed with canals which has served as the market garden of the city for centuries, a rare and beautiful, rural oasis minutes from the city's heart.

The great, Gothic heritage and splendour of Amiens is reflected elsewhere throughout the region: indeed, there is a profusion of fine, medieval towns rich in architecture and history which deserve to be visited. Laon, perched high on its outcrop of limestone, dominates the flat, broad plains of the Aisne below, the five towers of its Gothic cathedral soaring gracefully heavenward. Noyon's early Gothic cathedral, by contrast, is positively stout and powerful, its undecorated façade and heavy towers monumental and impressive if essentially down-to-earth. Senlis, a charming, walled, medieval town north of Paris, was a royal possession centuries ago, and the kings of France traditionally stopped here en route from Reims after their coronations. Its town centre remains intact and atmospheric, its delightful, twelfth-century cathedral remarkably delicate and beautiful with its graceful spire and its beautifully decorated central doorway.

Royal connections abound throughout the region. Compiègne was the site of several royal châteaux, the earliest dating from the ninth century when Charles the Bald built a modest palace and founded an abbey there. The château which can be visited today is altogether more formal and grand, a pompous, neo-classical edifice built in the eighteenth century by Louis XVI and refurbished by Napoleon. The nearby château of Chantilly is a similarly magnificent affair, the most beautiful in the region not simply for its Petit Château and Grand Château standing on an islet formed by the River Nonette but also for its formal gardens laid out by Le Nôtre, its magnificent Grandes Ecuries stables and, of course, its famous racecourse.

Such bucolic and pleasurable settings and activities belie the fact that Picardy is best remembered today, sadly, for its infamous killing fields and the destruction of its towns and cities in both world wars. Indeed, historically, this has been a region much fought over and not only in recent times. From Crécy, where Edward III defeated the French in 1346, across the centuries to the muddy trenches of the Somme and the more recent outrages that ravaged the towns and cities of Picardy during the Second World War: few other regions in France have suffered more.

Today, Picardy is at peace. From its brief stretch of coast around resorts like St-Valery-sur-Somme, across the wide, flat stretches of the Somme to the Thiérache tucked up against the national frontier with Belgium, through towns and cities charged with French history and to country spots where

Military cemetery

time seems hardly to exist: Picardy is a region full of charm, full of beauty which deserves to be visited.

à Table

Picardy cannot boast a strongly defined, regional cuisine but this, nonetheless, is a richly abundant region, the source of a wealth of fine produce and products which are utilized by chefs in simple *auberges* and grand restaurants alike. The *hortillonages* of Amiens are the most famous sources of fine, local vegetables but throughout the region there are scores of excellent market gardeners who work to ensure that good, fresh, seasonal produce finds its way into the kitchens of restaurants and hotel-restaurants alike. Picardy is also the source of excellent fruit: apples, pears and plums from the Thiérache, and especially red soft fruits from Noyon and its surrounding communities.

The Baie de la Somme yields superlative shellfish and fish. In truth, however, outside that coastal locality, fish merchants and restaurateurs are as likely as not to seek their raw materials from the much larger fish markets of Boulogne-sur-Mer in Pas de Calais or Dieppe in Upper Normandy. However, the Baie de la Somme remains the pre-eminent source of one of the region's undisputed delicacies, *pré-salé* lamb, that is, lamb which has grazed on the iodine-rich salt marshes of the bay. Also on the same salt

Baie de la Somme

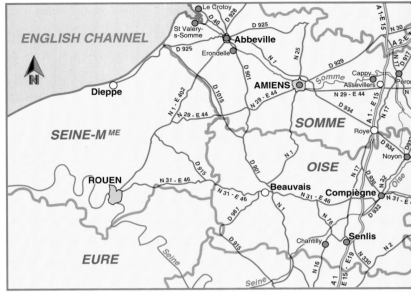

marshes, crafty and enterprising *pêcheurs à pied* search for a rich harvest of *haricots de mer* – samphire, a delicious sea vegetable which is an excellent, local accompaniment to fish dishes. Inland, the great forests of Compiègne and Le Nouvion yield, in season, an abundance of game including *chevreuil* (venison), *daguet* (young deer), *marcassin* (young wild boar), *bécasse* (woodcock), *faisan* (pheasant) and much else.

Maroilles, one of the great cheeses of northern France is produced in the Avesnois-Thiérache which overlaps both Picardy and Pas de Calais, so both regions can claim it as their own along with its attendant family of cheeses, Dauphin and Boulette d'Avesnes. Rollot is another fine, flavoursome, rind-washed cheese.

There are, furthermore, scores of goat's cheeses made in the region.

Restaurants in Picardy are not particularly strong on local or regional dishes with the exception of the ubiquitous *ficelle picarde*, a pancake filled with ham and a creamy sauce, covered with cheese and baked in the oven. Rather, the best seek instead to utilize the above produce and products in a repertoire that is with variations, of course, soundly based on *cuisine bourgeoise* traditions with only occasional daring forays into the more inventive. Yet, for our tastes this can be, at its best, French cuisine *par excellence*, boring and old hat perhaps for the jaded in search of new taste titillations, but for us often filling and satisfying after a day or two spent touring battlefields or cathedrals.

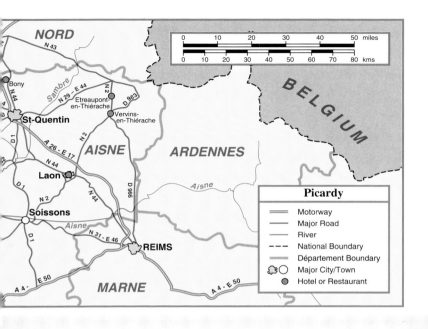

LE MENU DU TERROIR

soupe de l'hortillons
flamiche aux poireaux
pâté de canard en croute
ficelle picarde

anguille fumé
la cassolette de St-Jacques en feuilletage
sole meunière
haricots de mer

coq à la bière

agneau pré-salé de la Baie de la Somme
lapin au cidre

Maroilles
Dauphin
Boulette d'Avesnes
Rollot

sorbets des fruits rouges
macarons d'Amiens
crème chantilly

Small Hotels and Restaurants

80100 ABBEVILLE (SOMME)

Marché   Thur., last Wed. in month
Calais 113 km — Amiens 44 km — Boulogne-sur-Mer 79 km

RESTAURANT

Buffet de France
place de la Gare
tel.: 22 24 04 26
fax: 22 31 32 93

Abbeville is not a town we would stay in out of choice: not only was it almost completely destroyed in the last war, it is marred today by large-scale industry and the N1 which brings vast amounts of traffic trundling through it. The new bypass has helped to eliminate much of this, while the eventual completion of the Calais–Rouen *autoroute* should restore a degree of peace and some prosperity to its long-suffering residents. For those passing through Abbeville in need of a bite, the best place to head for is this excellent railway station restaurant-*brasserie*. The inexpensive menus represent superb value and the cuisine is a considerable notch above the merely adequate: local foods include a tasty *terrine de lapereau* and cod cooked in seaweed and raspberry vinegar.

Closed Wed. evening ❖ Credit cards: Visa/CB, Eurocard/Access ❖ Menus: 55 F (weekdays only), 80 F, 105 F, 140 F, 200 F ❖ à la carte: about 200 F

CHAMBRE D'HÔTE
AND *TABLE D'HÔTE*

8 km S.E. at
Erondelle

Manoir de La
Renardière
Château de la
Renardière
tel.: 22 27 13 00;
fax: 22 27 13 12

This ususual country mansion is located in the calm countryside of the Somme valley southeast of Abbeville. Here Madame Hélène Thaon d'Arnoldi offers superior *chambres*: six rooms are available with individual and personal, refined decor each with private bathroom and w.c. Some of the rooms have their own fireplaces, others have large French windows opening on to balconies that overlook the gardens. In the evenings, Madame d'Arnoldi offers a rather extravagant *table d'hôte* by reservation: candle-lit, gastronomic, four-course dinners based primarily on *fruits de mer* and fish.

Rooms: two persons 350–450 F including breakfast ❖ Table d'hôte: 250 F all inclusive ❖ Parking ❖ English spoken

80000 AMIENS (SOMME) 🛒

Marché Thur., Sat.

Festival *Fête des Hortillonages* third Sun. in June

Calais 140 km – 100 km Boulogne-sur-Mer – 114 km Rouen

HOTEL

Grand Hôtel de l'Univers

2, rue de Noyon

tel.: 22 91 52 51

fax: 22 92 81 66

Grand Hôtel de l'Univers, Amiens

This elegant, nineteenth-century *maison bourgeoise* in the heart of the cathedral city is, today, a friendly and personal, family-run, 3-star hotel owned by Monsieur and Madame Jean-Pierre Marteau. The building actually dates from 1850 and was originally constructed as a hotel at a time when Amiens was an important centre for the manufacture of fine velour. The hotel has forty-one sound-proofed bedrooms which have all been fully modernized and decorated pleasantly and each has private bathroom, w.c., satellite television, telephone and mini-bar. There is no restaurant but the Marteaus work with local specialists to supply *plateaux traiteur* which consists of full hot or cold meals served in the rooms. If you are going to arrive late and require this service, it would be advisable to telephone or fax for a menu so that your meal can be ready for your arrival. The hotel overlooks the pleasant St Denis gardens and is about ten minutes' walk from the cathedral.

Open all year ❖ Credit cards: Visa/ CB, Eurocard/Access, American Express, Diners ❖ Rooms: double 550 F, buffet breakfast 50 F ❖ Street parking as well as parking in nearby public garage ❖ Some English spoken ❖ L S H B

Small Hotels and Restaurants

RESTAURANT

Les Marissons
Pont de la Dodane
68, rue des Marissons
tel.: 22 92 96 66

Quartier St-Leu, Amiens

Amien's *quartier St-Leu*, crisscrossed with an intricate system of canals that branch off the Somme, was the town's centre of craft activity in the Middle Ages. Today, this lovely, old area has been transformed into its most pleasant neighbourhood, a quiet, stone-paved pedestrian area lined with restored houses, restaurants and bars along the waterside virtually within the shadow of the city's great and always dominating cathedral.

Les Marissons, located in a fifteenth-century boathouse, is probably the city's best restaurant and also one of its prettiest, especially in summer when you can enjoy an *apéritif* before your meal and coffee and *petits fours* afterwards in the lovely, flowered garden. Inside, the stylish dining room is decorated in shades of yellow and blue, the colours of Picardy, and the atmosphere is formal yet relaxing, almost soothing, with tables overlooking the water. Chef Antoine Benoit changes his menus every day depending on what he finds in the market but the emphasis is squarely on traditional, classic French *haute cuisine*. He is one of the few who still takes the trouble to make Amien's great speciality, *canard en croûte au foie gras préparé à la maison*. Other specialities include *nage d'écrevisses safrannées aux petits légumes*, a delicate and refined *hure de cervelle d'agneau aux poireaux sauce aux capres* and the sublime *joues de lotte rôties aux abricots*. There are excellent, local cheeses as well as some pretty, imaginative desserts. The wine list is extensive and, unusually, there is a good selection available by the glass.

Closed Sun. evening, Mon., and first half of Aug. ❖ Credit cards: Visa/CB, Eurocard/Access, American Express, Diners ❖ Menus: 135 F (weekdays only), 196 F, 235 F ❖ à la carte: about 320–350 F ❖ English spoken

RESTAURANT

Auberge du Vert Galant
57, chemin du Halage
tel.: 22 91 31 66

Amien's *hortillonages* lie just a few minutes' walk from the city centre, an extensive series of canals which crisscross a maze of rural plots and fields cultivated with fruit and vegetables. Migratory birds and waders nest in the reeds, and fishermen and hunters jealously guard their stretches of private waterfront.

Come here to relax and enjoy the peace of this rural waterland, all the more remarkable because of its location in the centre of a great city. The Vert Galant is a canal-side restaurant actually within the *hortillonages* where you can sit out by the water and enjoy essentially simple foods – *ficelle picarde, terrine picarde, flamiche de l'hortillons, saumon grillé, filet de canard* – as well as rent traditional boats for excursions through the canals. In truth, the food here is average at best, the service unhurried (if we are being generous): but the situation is so idyllic that you are prepared to make allowances. Otherwise, purchase some provisions, a Rollot cheese, a *baguette* or two and a bottle of wine, rent a boat, then strike out into the maze of canals to enjoy a *pique-nique dans les hortillonages*.

Closed Wed. evening, Sun. evening ❖ Credit cards: Visa/CB, Eurocard/Access, American Express, Diners ❖ Menus: 89 F, 179 F ❖ à la carte: about 150 F

Hortillonages, Amiens

02420 BONY (AISNE)
Calais 175 km – St-Quentin 18 km – Cambrai 25 km

FERME AUBERGE WITH
CHAMBRES D'HÔTE

**Ferme Auberge du
Vieux Puits**

5 bis, rue de l'Abbaye
tel.: 23 66 22 33

The Old Well farm at Bony lies in the heart of the
Vermandois countryside of Picardy and has been converted
into a welcoming *ferme auberge* with six well-equipped
chambres. Each room has private facilities, telephone and
satellite television. In the rustic dining room, Geneviève
Gyselinck serves guests traditional, home-cooked foods of
Picardy with fresh produce from the farm where possible.
Each day she bakes fresh bread and also makes traditional
terrines such as *terrine de lapereau aux noisettes* and *terrine de
foies de volaille*. Other specialities include *coq à la Picarde* and
canard picard aux groseilles sur reinettes dorées. Meals always
include *salade*, fresh vegetables and local cheeses and end
with home-cooked desserts such as Geneviève's prize-
winning *délice aux deux cousines et son coulis de mûres de ronces*.

Closed Thur., Sun. evening. Reservations advisable and appreciated ❖ Credit
card: Visa/CB ❖ Menus: 90 F, 150 F ❖ Rooms: one person 160 F, two persons
220 F including breakfast

80340 CAPPY (SOMME)
Calais 170 km – Péronne 16 km – A1 autoroute (exit 15) 10 km

RESTAURANT

L'Escale de Cappy

22, Chaussée Leon
Blum
tel.: 22 76 02 03
fax: 22 76 08 06

The Vallée de Haute Somme between Péronne and Amiens
is an atmospheric area of marshes and lakes which can
provide a pleasant and relaxing interlude for those driving
along the A1 *autoroute*. Stop here to enjoy lunch in this
lovely, country restaurant that is overflowing with flowers.
Here Claudie Seminet prepares an original *cuisine de terroir*,
utilizing local and regional products, often grouped around
a theme that varies with the seasons. Some of Claudie's
regional specialities include *feuilleté d'anguille et brochet*,
anguille fumée, flamiche aux poireaux, and *feuillantine de canard
samarobriva*.

Open daily lunchtimes, evenings Fri. and Sat.; closed 20 Dec.–10 Jan. ❖ Credit
card: Visa/CB ❖ Menus: 167 F, 236 F ❖ à la carte: about 250–300 F

60500 CHANTILLY (OISE) 🛒
Calais 250 km – Paris 41 km – Compiègne 44 km

HOTEL-RESTAURANT

**Hôtel-Gril
Campanile**
route de Creil
RN 16 Gouvieux
tel.: 44 57 39 24
fax: 44 58 10 05

We make no apologies if, from time to time, we include chain hotels in this guide. Chantilly's proximity to Paris attracts a well-heeled class of visitor and hotels and restaurants here are accordingly pricey. This reliable motel 3 kilometres north of the town is, therefore, useful. The rooms, admittedly, are no more than adequate: small, but each equipped with private bathroom and w.c., television, telephone, radio and coffee-making facilities. Additional beds can be supplied for children.

The young couple in charge, Véronique and Laurent Tamic, are helpful and welcoming and give the place the feel of a small, family-run hotel rather than that of a characterless, impersonal chain. The restaurant is really not bad at all, run in the typical Campanile style, with a blackboard in the dining room chalked up with daily specials prepared by Laurent. The menus are excellent value and there is always a wine of the month.

Open all year ❖ Credit cards: Visa/ CB, Eurocard/Access, American Express, Diners ❖ Rooms: double 268 F, buffet breakfast 28 F ❖ Menus: 80 F, 85 F (buffet), 100 F, menu enfant 39 F ❖ Parking

*Château
de Chantilly*

RESTAURANT-
BRASSERIE-
SALON DE THÉ

La Capitainerie
Château de Chantilly
tel.: 44 57 15 89

Chantilly's château is magnificently sited on an islet formed by the River Nonette and consists of two separate buildings, the sixteenth-century Petit Château and the adjoining Grand Château which was somewhat overzealously restored in 1880. The ancient, vaulted kitchens of the Petit Château, also known as the Capitainerie, have today been transformed into an informal *brasserie* and an atmospheric restaurant.

The *brasserie* is a useful if not overly exciting stop. The cafeteria-like atmosphere does not really take full advantage of the setting but the generous buffets of first courses and desserts, and the basically simple grills and *plats du jour*, are well-prepared and satisfying. The Restaurant Au Coin Gourmet, though, is noteworthy; open midday on weekends and holidays only, it is stylish and classic with beautifully laid tables which reflect the grandeur of the vaulted setting, and a menu that that takes no great risks but which is, nonetheless, interesting and appealing.

In the afternoons, coffee, tea, pastries and light snacks are served in the *brasserie* dining room.

Open lunch only (afternoon for salon de thé), closed Tue. Le Coin Gourmet Restaurant is open weekends and holidays only. ❖ Credit cards: Visa/ CB, Eurocard/Access, American Express, Diners ❖ Menus: Brasserie 75 F, 110 F, Restaurant Au Coin Gourmet 170 F ❖ à la carte: Brasserie about 100 F, Au Coin Gourmet about 220 F

La Capitainerie,
Château de Chantilly

Goûter Champêtre
Le Hameau
Parc du Château
tel.: 44 57 46 21

In 1775, Prince Louis de Condé created a wild, 'unspoilt' park beyond the girdled and constrained, formal gardens designed by Le Nôtre that surround the château, and here built for himself a rustic *hameau*, a Louis XVI style hamlet with a cluster of simple buildings where he would come to take light refreshments and, no doubt, idle away the hours.

Today, in the heart of the château park, actually beside the Prince's *hameau*, you can enjoy simple outdoor *goûters* of local picard specialities: *foie gras de canard, pâté de canard, lapin en gelée, tarte au cresson*, sandwiches of *rillettes de canard* or *magret de canard fumé*, accompanied by local cider, sparkling fruit wines or organic fruit juice. Meals finish with sensational fruit sorbets made by a cooperative of fruit growers near Noyon. The waiters and waitresses are young and friendly and wear period dress. This is a relaxing way to enjoy the château and its grounds. In case of rain, there is a tented pavilion in the garden.

*Goûter Champêtre,
Chantilly*

Open June–Sept. 1100–1900
❖ Credit cards: Visa/CB, Eurocard/Access ❖ Menu: 85 F ❖ à la carte: about 50–100 F

60200 COMPIÈGNE (OISE) 🛒
Marché   Wed., Sat.
Calais 220 km – Amiens 78 km – Arras 108 km

HOTEL-RESTAURANT

Hôtel de France-Restaurant Rôtisserie du Chat qui Tourne
17, rue Eugène Floquet
tel.: 44 40 02 74
fax: 44 40 48 37

This ancient, city centre inn, located on a small alley just down from Compiègne's magnificent Hôtel de Ville, does not quite date from the time when Jeanne d'Arc tried to raise the English siege of the town and was captured in the process, but it has been an inn since as long ago as 1665. At that time, it was known as the Hostellerie du Chat qui Tourne after a charlatan came to town and apparently gave a popular and impressive performance that included a cat roasting a chicken on a spit.

A 2-star *Logis de France*, the hotel has been in Madame Robert's family since the early part of the century. There are just twenty rooms, all off the central, winding staircase (there is no lift) which is lined with paintings that Madame has lovingly collected over the years. Rooms are atmospheric and comfortable: irregular in shape, with beamed ceilings and uneven floors, yet each is well equipped with bath or shower, w.c., television, telephone and mini-bar. Those rooms that have recently been redecorated have eye-soothing wallpaper and light, white furniture; those not yet redone are heavier in feel, dated undoubtedly yet full of character all the same.

The restaurant is well known locally. We find it charming, the dining room, with its lace tablecloths, crystal stemware, electric candles, floral curtains, and blue and yellow, velour decorations in the style of Louis XVI, the epitome of French provincial *par excellence*. Chef Vigogne serves honest, well-prepared, classic foods in generous abundance, presented with some style and imagination. Specialities include *terrine de foie gras de canard fait maison mariné au Loupiac, la cassolette de St-Jacques en feuilletage*, and *magret de canard rôti aux figues fraîches et sa galette de polenta*. Cheese is served with a bowl of salad, breads are homemade and desserts such as *gratin de fruits rouges et son sabayon* are excellent. The 145 F menu changes each week, while the 205 F menu changes monthly.

Hôtel de France, Compiègne

Open all year ❖ Credit cards: Visa/ CB, Eurocard/Access ❖ Rooms: double 320 F, breakfast 38 F ❖ Menus: 120 F, 145 F, 205 F, menu enfant 65 F ❖ à la carte: about 200 F ❖ Street parking or parking in nearby town square ❖ English and German spoken

BAR À VINS-
RESTAURANT

Le Bouchon

5, rue St-Martin

tel.: 44 40 05 32

This welcoming restaurant-cum-wine bar, located in Compiègne's medieval pedestrian area, is the best bet for a good, quick, inexpensive bite. In fine weather, sit at shaded, outdoor tables and enjoy basic, simple foods – drinking snacks such as ham or cheese *tartines*, the daily *plat du jour*, or else a plate of *foie gras maison* or an *andouillette grillé*, washed down by an excellent selection of wines available by the glass or bottle.

Closed Sun., Mon. ❖ Credit cards: Visa/CB, Eurocard/Access, American Express, Diners ❖ à la carte: about 75–100 F, plat du jour 48 F

80500 LE CROTOY (SOMME) 🛒

Marché Tues., Fri.

Calais 98 km – Abbeville 26 km – Boulogne-sur-Mer 64 km

RESTAURANT
WITH ROOMS

**Hôtel de la Baie-
Restaurant Mado**

quai Léonard

tel.: 22 27 80 42
   22 27 81 42

Chez Mado is a famous, old eating house on the waterfront of Le Crotoy, a rather quiet and out of the way resort and fishing village on the Baie de la Somme across from the much livelier and more frequented St-Valery-sur-Somme. Jeanne d'Arc was held in prison here before being taken across the bay by boat to St-Valery en route to Rouen, and a statue of the maiden warrior in chains commemorates this.

Le Crotoy

Madame Mado, by all accounts almost as formidable a *grande dame* herself, has now retired but this popular restaurant certainly shows no sign of running out of *vapeur*. The new porch, though less atmospheric than the magpie decoration of the formal dining room, has tables that overlook the waterfront and the vast salt marshes of the Baie de la Somme across to St-Valery. Come here to enjoy a 120 F menu which is remarkably generous and carefully prepared: first a nibble of sweet *crevettes grises* from the bay to whet the appetite, then either a huge bowl of steaming *moules marinières* or a tureen of richly concentrated *soupe de poissons*, followed by excellent *sole meunière* or *lieu au moutarde à l'ancienne*. The main courses are served with fresh samphire from the marshes (here called *haricots de mer*), and homemade noodles. Meals are rounded off with either a selection of cheeses or rounds of hot goat's cheese served with a small salad followed by a good selection of homemade desserts. House wine, Côte de Buzet *blanc*, *rosé* or *rouge*, is excellent at 65 F.

There are only three rooms which are always in great demand. They were occupied when we visited so we could not inspect them. However, all three benefit from outstanding views across the bay and have full private facilities.

Open daily all year ❖ Credit cards: Visa/CB, Eurocard/Access ❖ Menus: 120 F, 170 F ❖ à la carte: about 150 F ❖ Rooms: 300–350 F ❖ English spoken

---

02580 ETREAUPONT-EN-THIÉRACHE (AISNE)
Calais 260 km – Laon 44 km – St-Quentin 51 km

HOTEL

Hôtel Le Clos du Montvinage
RN 2
tel.: 23 97 40 18
    23 97 91 10
fax: 23 97 48 92

Monsieur and Madame Trokay have run the well-known Auberge du Val de l'Oise (see below) for nearly twenty years but they only opened this 3-star *Logis de France* hotel just up the road from the restaurant in 1987. This splendid, nineteenth-century mansion on the old road between Paris and Brussels makes an excellent base for exploring the Thiérache or the nearby Avesnois countryside, relatively unknown areas of unspoiled, rural France, dotted with farms, typical towns and villages and impressive, characteristic, fortified churches.

Madame Marie-Lise Trokay is a charming and vivacious

hostess and she has decorated her hotel with considerable style. The twenty bedrooms are all simply furnished in shades of blue, pink or green; they are comfortable and well equipped, each with a private bath or shower, w.c., satellite television, telephone, mini-bar and hair dryer. Most of the rooms enjoy a pleasant outlook over the lovely, lawned gardens. There is a mezzanine room which is ideal for families, as well as a ground-floor room converted for the disabled. The breakfast room is very typically French, and there is a comfortable bar with French billiards. Sporting facilities in the hotel include two 'tentkit' courts (a sort of short tennis), bicycles, croquet in the garden and table tennis.

Closed Sun. ❖ Credit cards: Visa/CB, Eurocard/Access, American Express, Diners ❖ Rooms: double 305–355 F, breakfast 35 F ❖ Parking ❖ English and Spanish spoken

---

RESTAURANT

Auberge du Val de l'Oise

RN 2

tel.: 23 97 40 18

23 97 91 10

fax: 23 97 48 92

While Madame Trokay busies herself in their charming hotel down the road, her husband is happiest continuing to please old and new customers alike in this atmospheric and fine restaurant located in an *ancien relais de poste*. Monsieur Trokay's establishment is highly acclaimed for its use of fresh, local ingredients put together in inventive and creative ways. There are two dining rooms, one in the Picardy style with dark beams and a large fireplace, the other in the style of a turn of the century *bistro*. Monsieur Trokay does the cooking himself and his specialities include *tarte au Maroilles, lapeareau au cidre, ris de veau à la vieille prune et aux cèpes* and *poêle de St-Jacques au coulis d'oursins*. In season, he makes plentiful use of the excellent game from the surrounding area.

Closed Sun. evening, Mon. midday ❖ Credit cards: Visa/CB, Eurocard/Access, American Express, Diners ❖ Menus: 75 F (weekdays only), 120 F, 130 F, 170 F (including wine), 210 F, menu enfant 60 F ❖ à la carte: about 150–200 F ❖ English and Spanish spoken

02000 LAON (AISNE) 🍴

Calais 220 km – Amiens 120 km – Reims 58

HOTEL-RESTAURANT

Hôtel de la
Bannière de France
11, rue Franklin-
Roosevelt
tel.: 23 23 21 44
fax: 23 23 21 44

Laon is a magnificent hill town that dominates the surrounding dull and flat countryside, its Gothic cathedral visible from afar like a great ship serenely riding the crest of an immense wave. While the new town lies below within easy access of the A26 *autoroute*, old Laon clusters around its cathedral in a maze of small and narrow streets.

This *ancien relais de poste* is located in the atmospheric *haute ville* a five-minute walk from the cathedral. Dating from 1685, it is an historic hotel that now combines 3-star comfort with atmosphere. The eighteen rooms are all tastefully decorated, light, airy and spacious and each has private bathroom, w.c., satellite television and telephone. There is a private garage for parking as well as public parking on the street behind the hotel.

We like the solidly classical, traditional restaurant. The long dining room with its pink walls and simple, white tablecloths, fresh flowers on the tables, wooden floor and ladder chairs is tastefully sober without being overly formal. The cuisine is neither especially exciting nor innovative but it is quietly satisfying nonetheless: *terrine de ris de veau, panaché de poisson aux petits légumes, turbot poêlé à la coriandre.*

For those heading north or south on the A26 en route to or from the Channel Tunnel, the Bannière makes a useful and enjoyable stopover.

Closed 20 Dec.–20 Jan., 1 May
❖ Credit cards: Visa/CB, Eurocard/
Access, American Express, Diners
❖ Rooms: double 360 F, breakfast 35 F
❖ Menus: 112 F, 160 F, 300 F, menu
enfant 48 F ❖ à la carte: about 200–
250 F ❖ Parking in private garage
❖ English, German and Spanish
spoken

Hôtel de la Bannière de France, Laon

60400 NOYON (OISE) 🛒

Festival *Marché de Fruits Rouges* second Sun. in July
Calais 200 km – Compiègne 24 km – Laon 52 km

HOTEL-RESTAURANT

**Hôtel Restaurant
St-Eloi**

81, boulevard Carnot
tel.: 44 44 01 49
fax: 44 09 20 90

Noyon, today a rather quiet market town most notable for its surrounding soft fruit orchards, was an important bishopric in medieval days. Charlemagne was crowned here in 768 and the puritanical John Calvin was born in the town in 1509. Today, the main reason for coming here is to enjoy a rather quiet, provincial town which boasts one of the great, Gothic cathedrals of the region. Twenty thousand enthusiastic visitors also descend on Noyon each year in mid-July for the *marché de fruits rouges* festival.

Another reason for stopping in Noyon is simply to enjoy the warm hospitality of Monsieur and Madame Jean-Pierre Jouve, an extremely friendly couple who took over the 2-star hotel, located in a traditional, nineteenth-century house, just a few years ago after running a hotel in Normandy near Bayeux for over a decade.

The hotel has been completely renovated although at the moment there are only two spacious, de luxe rooms in the main house, beautifully furnished, well equipped and full of character. The remaining sixteen rooms are located in an adjoining, modern wing that overlooks a quiet, secluded court-yard. Smaller, furnished with reproduction pieces, each is well equipped with a modern bathroom, w.c., television and telephone: but they lack any real character, a disappointment given that the main building is quite interesting and grand.

Come here, all the same, to enjoy Madame Jouve's classic cuisine in menus that change with the seasons. The pastel dining room, with its high ceiling and tables laid with crystal and porcelain, is rather formal like the cuisine itself: specialities include *pâté en croûte de canard farci au foie gras, queues de langoustines au chou vert et lardons, truite de mer sur lit d'oseille, lapin aux pruneaux, magret de canard en éventail sauce cassis* and homemade *pâtisseries* and desserts.

Closed Sun. evening, and 1–21 Aug. ❖ Credit cards: Visa/CB, American Express ❖ Rooms: double 290 F, de luxe room 480 F, breakfast 35 F ❖ Menus: 130 F, 160 F, 200 F, menu enfant on request ❖ à la carte: about 250 F ❖ Parking ❖ English spoken

Small Hotels and Restaurants

HOTEL-RESTAURANT

**Hôtel-Restaurant
Le Cèdre**
8, rue de l'Evêché
tel.: 44 44 23 24
fax: 44 09 53 79

The brick architecture of this modern, 2-star hotel does not do much for us – it is almost like a large stable block – but the most noteworthy and remarkable feature about Le Cèdre is its superlative location opposite Noyon's imposing, twelfth-century cathedral. The hotel is just four years old and was constructed over ancient Roman ramparts that were uncovered during its construction and which can still be seen in the basement. There are thirty-four modern rooms, all identical, each with private bath, w.c., television and telephone. The Restaurant L'Entrecôte serves a range of good value menus – for 120 F, for example, you can enjoy *mousse de brocoli au crabe*, then either *truite en papillote sauce Champagne* or *confit de canard*, followed by cheese and dessert – as well as nicely presented *salades composées*. You are quite welcome to come here for a full meal or just for a salad or an omelette. The management, under owner Monsieur Michel Courtier, is friendly and helpful.

Open all year ❖ Credit cards: Visa/CB, Eurocard/Access ❖ Rooms: double 290 F, buffet breakfast 38 F ❖ Menus: 69 F, 90 F, 120 F, 180 F, menu enfant 35 F ❖ à la carte: about 150 F ❖ Parking ❖ English and Spanish spoken ❖ L S H B

80200 PÉRONNE (SOMME)
Calais 170 km – Amiens 51 km – St-Quentin 30 km

HOTEL-RESTAURANT

Hôtel Mercure
Aire d'Assevillers
A1 autoroute
tel.: 22 84 12 76
fax: 22 85 28 92

This conveniently situated *autoroute* hotel just off the A1 is included for one reason only: anyone heading north or south on the *autoroute* in need of an overnight stop should consider Péronne, a historic town located in the heart of the First World War Somme battlefield. In a modern building in the grounds of the château is the *Historial de la Grande Guerre*, an important and moving museum dedicated to the First World War which should on no account be missed if you are passing through this area.

The Mercure's forty-five rooms are spacious, pleasantly decorated if modern and by definition uniform; they are soundproofed and well equipped, each with private bathroom and w.c., air conditioning, satellite television, telephone and mini-bar. The Restaurant Les Anguillères serves some regional foods including *ficelle picarde, anguille fumée à la crème d'herbes* and the ubiquitous *flamiche aux poireaux*. Otherwise, stick to the grills to be on the safe side.

Open all year ❖ Credit cards: Visa/CB, Eurocard/Access, American Express, Diners ❖ Rooms: 360– 495 F ❖ Menus: 125 F, menu enfant 49 F ❖ à la carte: about 120 F ❖ Parking ❖ English spoken

---

80230 ST-VALERY-SUR-SOMME (SOMME)

Marché Sun.

Calais 108 km – Abbeville 18 km – Boulogne-sur-Mer 67 km

HOTEL-RESTAURANT

Le Relais Guillaume de Normandy

46, quai du Romerel

tel.: 22 60 82 36

fax: 22 60 81 82

Unlike most coastal towns in this area, St-Valery-sur-Somme, which served as a German command centre during the Second World War, escaped from that conflict virtually unscathed. Consequently, it still enjoys a rather charming, old-fashioned (if somewhat faded) feel which we find delightful, especially compared to ugly and characterless, purpose-built resorts that were created after the war, like the ghastly sprawl of nearby Fort-Mahon-Plage.

This house from the turn of the century located at the end of the *quai*, probably the most atmospheric and comfortable house on the waterfront, is today a 2-star hotel-restaurant. There are fourteen rooms, each with private bath or shower, w.c., satellite television and telephone, but the best feature, and one worth paying extra for, is the outstanding view over the salt marshes of the bay. The restaurant is good, too, if not overly exciting or exceptional. Still, the 85 F

Le Relais Guillaume de Normandy, St-Valery-sur-Somme

menu has those regional specialities which you come to St-Valery to enjoy, either a richly concentrated *soupe de poisson maison* or the regional *ficelle picarde*, followed by *agneau pré-salé de la Baie*, lamb which has grazed on the salt marshes, so imparting a rather gamey, iodiney flavour to the meat.

Credit cards: Visa/CB, Eurocard/Access ❖ Rooms: double 250–300 F, breakfast 35 F ❖ Menus: 85 F, 160 F, 195 F, menu enfant 45 F ❖ à la carte: about 200–250 F ❖ Parking

---

HOTEL-RESTAURANT

Hôtel-Restaurant du Port et des Bains
1, quai Blavet
tel.: 22 60 80 20

The Port is probably the best fish restaurant in town for value for money according to both locals and regular visitors alike. The Port is located on the waterfront and the two large dining rooms fill up quickly, so be sure to reserve your midday table well in advance on weekends and holidays. There is a very typical ambiance that can only be described as *très française* in the dining room, with Madame presiding over the banks of tables laid with crisp, white cloths. On a midday in early summer the windows were steamed up which ensured that neither the passing crowds nor the view of salt marshes in the bay could distract from the serious business of eating. We joined the locals and French families on holiday, rolled up our sleeves and tucked into the 98 F menu which offered a range of ten different fishy starters including *praires farci, huîtres, moules marinières, soupe de poissons* and *marinade de saumon*, followed by excellent fried sole and a *brochette de poissons* then cheese and dessert.

The 1-star hotel has a number of simple, extremely basic but comfortable rooms, some with private shower and w.c., and outstanding views across the bay.

Credit cards: Visa/CB, Eurocard/Access ❖ Menus: 45 F, 82 F, 98 F, 145 F, 175 F ❖ à la carte: about 150 F ❖ Rooms: double 160–200 F

RESTAURANT

Relais des 4 Saisons
2, place Croix-l'Abbé
tel.: 22 26 94 85

When St-Valery is crowded it is *really* crowded. Escape to the always quieter fortified *vieille ville*, then, if you're feeling peckish, carry on up to this pleasant, modern, ivy-covered, roadside inn which serves stylish and well-presented cuisine at reasonable prices. The 85 F menu offers *salade de taboulé aux fruits de mer, aile de raie au vinaigre de framboise, fromage* and dessert. There are some excellent, reasonably priced wines such as Sauvignon de Touraine for 45 F. After lunch, seek out the nearby Chapelle des Marins, sited in the middle of a field overlooking the Somme.

Closed Sun. evening, Mon. (except holidays) ❖ Credit cards: Visa/CB, Eurocard/Access, American Express, Diners ❖ Menus: 85 F, 125 F, 145 F, menu enfant 40 F ❖ à la carte: about 175–200 F

CHAMBRE D'HÔTE

Madame Claire Sauvage

22, quai du Romerel

tel.: 22 60 80 98

Madame Claire Sauvage has lived in this century-old, traditional house on St-Valery's waterfront since 1945 when she and her husband reclaimed his family home after five years of German occupation. Previously, St-Valery was a quiet agricultural and fishing town: tourism came much later, perhaps because the town escaped damage in the war. Today, with its yacht marina, steam train and scores of restaurants, St-Valery is probably the most popular place on Picardy's coast. Come to Madame Sauvage's house to experience something of St-Valery as it used to be. Indeed,

though in the centre of town on the *quai*, it is still peaceful here and makes a lovely base for exploring the area. Madame Sauvage offers four large, traditionally furnished rooms, two with private bath and w.c., two with shower and w.c. Ask for a room with a view of the marshes and the Baie de la Somme.

Rooms: two persons 270 F including breakfast ❖ Parking

Chambre d'hôte

Small Hotels and Restaurants

BISTRO

Le Bistro 191
9, rue Léon Fautrat
tel.: 44 53 68 88

Senlis is a fine, medieval town just off the A1 *autoroute* not far from Paris. It is certainly worth stopping here to see the magnificent, twelfth-century, Gothic cathedral, the vestiges of the Gallo-Roman ramparts, and to walk along its old, cobbled and atmospheric streets.

This simple, casual *bistro* makes a welcome and informal midday stop. Centrally located in the old town just a few

minutes from the cathedral, it serves excellent, traditional foods: *œufs en meurette, museau en vinaigrette, salade aux lardons* followed by *escalope normande, pavé sauce roquefort, rognons à la moutarde.* Complete the meal with a slab of Brie de Meaux or a warm slice of homemade *tarte*. The wine list, though reasonably priced, is imprecise, so ask for advice or try the *sélection du mois.*

Closed Mon. evening, Tue. ❖ Credit cards: Visa/CB, Eurocard/Access ❖ à la carte: about 150 F

Senlis

02140 VERVINS-EN-THIÉRACHE (AISNE)
Calais 250 km – Laon 43 km – Reims 70 km

HOTEL-RESTAURANT

La Tour du Roy

45, rue du Général
Leclerc
tel.: 23 98 00 11
fax: 23 98 00 72

The marvellous, turreted manor house midway between Paris and Brussels was where Henry IV of France received news of his accession to the throne in 1598. Today, it is a luxurious, fully renovated hotel with a superlative restaurant. The twenty rooms are well appointed, each with private bath and w.c., telephone, mini-bar, satellite television, and are furnished individually and atmospherically. A few have terraces and balconies overlooking the splendid gardens, while the most distinctive, unique and expensive (named Henri IV and Sire de Coucy) are located in the medieval towers themselves.

The proprietor, Madame Annie Desvignes, oversees the kitchen herself and is famous for her repertoire of regional and classic dishes presented in a particularly light, inventive and elegant manner that has earned her a Michelin rosette. Some of her specialities include *rémoulade de coquilles St-Jacques*, *huîtres gratinées en sabayon de paprika sur salades braisées*, *pigeonneau rôti au gingembre*, and a wonderfully light and airy *soufflé au whisky*. The *spécialités du terroir* menu at 160 F or 200 F including wine is particularly recommended. Monsieur Claude Desvignes is in charge of the cellar and he is as enthusiastic and knowledgeable about wines as he is about his native Thiérache: he delights in helping visitors to further their discoveries of this lovely area.

Restaurant closed Sun. evening, Mon. midday, and mid–Jan. to mid–Feb.
❖ Credit cards: Visa/CB, Eurocard/Access, American Express, Diners
❖ Rooms: double 350–450 F, de luxe suites 600–800 F, breakfast 60 F
❖ Menus: 160 F (200 F including wine), 280 F, 400F (including Champagne), menu enfant 80 F ❖ à la carte: about 350–400 F ❖ Parking ❖ English spoken
❖ L S H B

103

CHAMPAGNE

Champagne is the wine region closest to the Channel Tunnel, a mere three hours from Calais by way of the A26 *autoroute* which leads directly to the heart of the wine country. A short break in this region, which gives the world its finest and most elegant sparkling wine, is a more than feasible and enjoyable proposition.

Today, vineyards cover only a small part of the former province of Champagne, extending primarily across the slight ridge of hills optimistically called the Montagne de Reims between Reims and Epernay, along the Vallée de la Marne into

Picardy, and south of Epernay in an area known as the Côte des Blancs because of the predominance of the white grape Chardonnay. As the region is on the far edge of the area covered by this book, we have concentrated on the heart of the wine country located in the *département* of the Marne.

Reims and Epernay are the two great towns of Champagne and wine lovers may certainly wish to visit both, not least to tour famous Champagne houses whose underground *caves* carved out of soft, white chalk extend for literally hundreds of kilometres

La Champagne

beneath their streets. Reims is the capital of the region in every sense, a large, bustling and modern metropolis that suffered severe damage during both world wars. Monuments from the past give a vivid impression of the magnitude and importance of the *ville-sainte*, the sacred city, where the kings of France almost without exception came to be crowned and consecrated.

Reims may well be the capital of Champagne, the region, but Epernay is unquestionably the capital of Champagne, the wine. Come to this much smaller and more manageable town for no other reason than to enjoy Champagne: to visit as many of the *grandes marques* as you care to; to sample Champagne by the *coupe*, *flûte* or bottle in city cafés and bars or on a vineyard *pique-nique* while touring one of the signposted *Routes du Champagne*; or simply to luxuriate in fine hotels located in the city centre or in outlying districts amidst the vineyards, where the great wines of Champagne are impeccably partnered in elegance by a fine *haute cuisine champenoise*.

The region that gives the world a wine that is at once the epitome of luxury, frivolity, elegance, sheer joy, happiness, even decadence, is itself surprisingly sober, its quiet wine villages introverted, silent, even a little grey. Appearances may be deceptive, however: for whether below ground in *caves*, in elegant country hotels and restaurants or in simple *chambres d'hôtes* and *fermes auberges*, the radiance of Champagne, the wine, is reflected in the warmth and generosity of the champenois people. There is nothing

even remotely snooty about the region and Champagne itself is a wine that, while always valued, is, nonetheless, taken remarkably for granted, to be enjoyed generously and in quantity at virtually any time of the day. What better reason to visit?

à Table

Nowhere is the essential and fascinating contrast between Champagne the region and Champagne the wine more apparent than in the cuisine. For indeed, while the true foods of Champagne are a reflection of a rustic and hard-working country, at the same time, the image of Champagne as the world's most elegant and luxurious wine has demanded that within the region itself a *haute cuisine champenoise* has developed. Typical and authentic *champenois* foods, for example, include *salade de pissenlits aux lardons* (young, wild dandelion leaves dressed with hot bacon fat and strips of bacon), *andouillettes de Troyes* (a particularly forthright example of that 'gutsy' favourite), *pieds de porc à la Ste-Ménéhould* (pig's trotters poached until tender, boned, then rolled in breadcrumbs and sizzled under a hot grill), or the *potée champenoise*, a simmering cauldron filled with cured pork, sausage, cabbage, potatoes, turnips and anything else you might care to throw in. These, clearly, are not the sort of foods that you immediately think of as an accompaniment to Champagne.

Understandably, in the scores of superlative restaurants in city and country alike, a most special and superb cuisine has evolved utilizing the

fine produce and products of the region.
Prepared classically or innovatively,
sometimes utilizing Champagne and
marc de Champagne, it is presented
elegantly and with considerably style
in refined dining rooms that truly
are a reflection of the prestige that
Champagne has brought to the region.

LE MENU DU TERROIR

salade aux lardons
jambonneau de Reims
foie gras d'oie au ratafia
escargots fraises de Champagne

mousseline de brochet au Champagne
matelote des bords de la Marne braisée au Champ.
salade tiède de St-Jacques au foie gras chaud

pieds de porc à la Ste-Ménéhould
civet de lapin fermier
potée champenoise
filet de bœuf à la moëlle et au Bouzy
poulet au Champagne

feuilleté de Maroilles
Brie de Meaux
Chaource
Langres
Coulommiers

sorbet au marc de Champagne
mousse de fruits au Champagne
biscuits roses de Reims

Royal Champagne, Champillon Bellevue

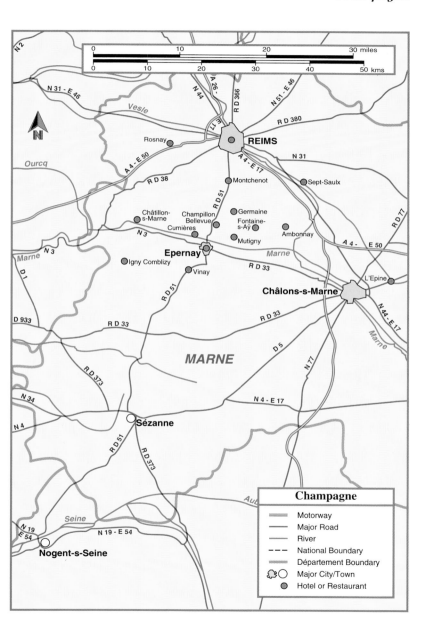

Small Hotels and Restaurants

51150 AMBONNAY (MARNE) 🍴

Calais 311 km – Reims 29 km – Epernay 20 km

HOTEL-RESTAURANT

Auberge St-Vincent

1, rue St-Vincent

tel.: 26 57 01 98

fax: 26 57 81 48

Ambonnay is an extremely quiet, typical wine village located in the heart of the Grand Cru vineyards of the Montagne de Reims about midway between Reims and Epernay. The Auberge St-Vincent, a small, simple, 2-star *Logis de France*, is an old favourite of ours. Monsieur and Madame Pelletier are welcoming hosts. The ten rooms are comfortable, if on the small side, and they have all been recently refurbished and decorated, each with private bath, w.c., telephone and television.

The best reason for coming here, whether or not you are spending the night, is to enjoy the superlative restaurant which serves the authentic country foods of Champagne, carefully researched, prepared and presented by Jean-Claude Pelletier. Typical foods on the four-course 170 F *menu champenois* include *salade St-Vincent* (served in a Champagne bottle that has been sawed in half), *la cassolette de petits gris, boudin de lapin champenois, petite langue confite au ratafia, feuilleté de Maroilles, sorbet au marc de Champagne*. These are not fussy or finnicky foods; rather, this is a full-flavoured and genuine cuisine of the country and we find it simply delicious and satisfying. Do such foods go with Champagne, you may ask? In fact, we consider the full-flavoured house Champagne from Ambonnay to be more than a match. But if you are in doubt, try a bottle of still Bouzy *rouge* instead.

Breakfast is served in a pleasant room decorated with Champagne barrels and tools, and there is a bar much patronized by the local wine growers.

Closed Sun. evening, Mon., and Feb. ❖ Credit cards: Visa/CB, Eurocard/ Access, American Express, Diners ❖ Rooms: double 290–360 F, breakfast 35 F ❖ Menus: 130 F, 170 F, 240 F, 290 F, menu enfant 40 F ❖ à la carte: about 300 F ❖ English spoken

51160 CHAMPILLON BELLEVUE (MARNE)

Calais 315 km – Epernay 6 km – Reims 20 km

HOTEL-RESTAURANT

**Domaine Royal
Champagne**
RN 51
tel.: 26 52 87 11

The Royal Champagne, named after the regiment that looked after the French king, is a magnificent, eighteenth-century *relais de la poste* located just outside Epernay along the old royal road by which the kings travelled to Reims for their coronations. It is highly probable that they paused here for refreshment; indeed, Napoleon himself spent the night here when he visited his old army cadet chum, Claude Moët.

Today, this prestigious, 4-star member of the Relais & Châteaux group of independent hotels is actually owned by Moët & Chandon and is quite simply one of the great hotels of the region, a magnificent and peaceful place to stay, literally amidst the vineyards. The reception and dining room are located in the main, old coaching inn. Decorated with military paraphanalia, maps, swords and a pair of boots that surely would have been far too large for Napoleon himself, this is an atmospheric and historic spot. The dining room itself is rustic, a high-beamed room with a large bay window that opens out on to an incredible view of the vineyards. A huge fireplace gives it the air of something like an old hunting lodge. Here you can enjoy at your leisure a refined *haute cuisine champenoise* prepared by young chef Christophe Blot. His style is classic, his touch light and sure: typical specialities include *escargots de Champagne en robe des champs, royale de perche aux baies de genièvre tombée de choux braisé reduction de Bouzy, jarret de veau à l'ancienne* and *poularde de Bresse en chemise de persil et d'ail cuite sous croute de sel*. Local cheeses include Langres, Coulommiers and Chaource. The wine list is, of course, rightly dominated by Champagnes and there are a number of reasonably priced examples from both small growers and large houses.

The twenty-five bedrooms are located below the main building in two terraces of modern bungalows which overlook the vineyards. In a sense, this is something like a super de luxe motel because you can park virtually in front of your room. The rooms are named individually and are entered from an external corridor. They are all large, beautiful, tastefully furnished and luxuriously appointed. They are most noteworthy for their magnificent views over

the vineyards extending to the Côte des Blancs beyond
Epernay. The position of the Royal Champagne is quite
exceptional and unrivalled.

If you wish to visit Champagne producers ask at
reception and they will assist in arranging appointments.

Open all year ❖ Credit cards: Visa/CB,
Eurocard/Access, American Express,
Diners ❖ Rooms: 600–1350 F (20%
discount in low season) ❖ Menus:
175 F (weekdays only), 250 F, 350 F,
400 F ❖ à la carte: about 400–500 F
❖ Parking ❖ English, German and
Spanish spoken ❖ L S H B

*Chef Christophe Blot, Royal
Champagne, Champillon
Bellevue*

51700 CHÂTILLON-SUR-MARNE (MARNE) 🛒

Marché Wed.
Calais 314 km – Epernay 19 km – Reims 32 km

RESTAURANT

La Porte Oubliée
6, place Urban II
tel.: 26 58 37 58

One of the most dominant and striking landmarks in the
Vallée de la Marne is the immense statue to Pope Urban II,
who was born here in 1042, and who as pope initiated the
First Crusade in 1095. It is worth coming up here for the
sensational views over the vineyards of the Marne.
Afterwards, repair to this small, locally popular restaurant
which serves solid, if not overly distinguished, traditional
foods: specialities include *foie gras maison, noix de St-Jacques à*

l'éffiloché d'endive, suprême de volaille au Champagne, coq au vin des Coteaux Champenois.

Closed Mon., second half of Aug.
❖ Menus: 60 F (weekdays only), 90 F, 140 F, 180 F ❖ à la carte: about 200 F

*Pope Urban II,
Châtillon-sur-Marne*

51480 CUMIÈRES (MARNE) 🛒
Calais 311 km – Epernay 3 km

RESTAURANT

Le Caveau

tel.: 26 54 83 23

fax: 26 54 24 56

The great, hidden heritage of the Champagne region is its network of *caves* which literally extend for hundreds of kilometres beneath the streets of both Reims and Epernay as well as underneath even the most modest, rural wine village. Cumières is typical, a small commune of just 800 inhabitants but with over eighty individual *récoltants-manipulants* each with their own often deep and surprisingly extensive system of *caves* extending beneath their houses.

One such old Champagne *cave* on the edge of town has been put to a different but no less welcome use: here at Le Caveau, Jean-Claude Rambach has created one of the most atmospheric, pleasant and welcoming restaurants in the area, actually sited within a *cave* some 17 metres underground. You don't actually have to descend that far – the *cave* burrows into a chalk cliff face under the vineyards of Hautvillers above. The damp, sometimes moist, chalk walls provide a cool respite from the oppressive heat of summer, while the temperature remains constant even in the cold of winter. There is an intimate and cosy atmosphere here. The tables are all lit by candles in Champagne bottles separated from each other by *pupitres*, and the waiters are dressed in traditional *champenois* dress.

Jean-Claude is a serious chef and he offers a considered but essentially classic *cuisine champenoise* that utilizes the

111

best, local, seasonal produce and products. The menus change each fortnight: local wine growers and businessmen come in at midday during the week to enjoy a good, inexpensive menu of 85 F that might include *salade du caveau* followed by *fricassée de poulet aux champignons, fromage* and *dessert*. The 150 F menu, on the other hand, is more serious: *feuilleté d'escargots aux petits champignons*, a break for the *trou champenois*, then a hearty plate of *confit de canard aux morilles* or a grilled *faux-filet aux petits oignons frais*, a selection of local cheeses, then a choice of homemade desserts. The 250 F *menu surprise* comprises seven different small dishes which Jean-Claude devises depending on what is fresh that day at market. Champagnes are reasonably priced (Henri Abelé 175 F) but give thought, too, to trying the excellent red Coteaux Champenois wines of Cumières, which are some of the best in the region in our opinion.

Incidentally, Jean-Claude is the regional *connetable* of the *Confrerie du Sabre d'Or*: thus if you would like to try your hand at opening a bottle of Champagne by decapitating the top of the bottle with a sabre, he will be happy to teach you how to do so safely and expertly, and afterwards present you with a certificate.

Closed Sun. evening, Mon. ❖ Credit cards: Visa/CB, Eurocard/Access, American Express ❖ Menus: 85 F (weekdays lunch only), 150 F, 198 F, 250 F ❖ à la carte: about 200 F

Jean-Claude Rambach,
Le Caveau, Cumières

51206 EPERNAY (MARNE) 🛒

Marché   Tue., Sat.

Calais 306 km – Reims 26 km – Paris 143 km

HOTEL-RESTAURANT-
WINE BAR

Hôtel Les Berceaux

13, rue des Berceaux

tel.: 26 55 28 84

fax: 26 55 10 36

Les Berceaux,
Epernay

This old favourite is still the best base in town, a comfortable, 3-star hotel-restaurant owned and run personally by Luc and Jill Maillard. Located in the centre of Epernay, a five-minute walk from the prestigious Avenue de Champagne, home of some of Champagne's most famous producers, Les Berceaux is certainly the place to come to gain at first hand a more than passing acquaintance with the world's greatest sparkling wine. Start off immediately with a *coupe* or two in the hotel wine bar where Luc always keeps at least three or four Champagnes open to sample by the glass.

The accommodation at Les Berceaux is adequate if not overly distinguished, the rooms homely and comfortable rather than luxurious. There are twenty-nine, each with private bath or shower, w.c., television and telephone. For such a small town, Epernay is surprisingly hectic and busy,

and the hotel's central location does mean that some rooms can suffer from excessive traffic noise.

Luc is a native of Champagne, Jill is English, and this rare combination really sparkles. They, and the young team that they have assembled, know how to make their guests comfortable and will go out of their way to help in any way. As a significant, added bonus, Luc is himself the chef of the excellent and highly regarded restaurant. His is basically a classic cuisine that utilizes, above all, the fine, fresh ingredients and produce of the region. Notable specialities include *la cassolette d'escargots au Champagne, coquilles St-Jacques aux légumes* and good duck breast cooked in red wine. The Champagne list, incidentally, is one of the best we have encountered anywhere and prices even for *grandes marques* are extremely reasonable.

In contrast to the more formal atmosphere of the restaurant, the Maillard's wine bar is casual and informal, a lovely, *belle époque* ambiance which leads to easy conviviality over a *coupe* or several of Champagne. You can come here simply for a drink or to enjoy basically simple *bistro*-type foods together with a range of Champagnes and other wines by the glass or bottle.

Restaurant closed Sun. evening ❖ Credit cards: Visa/CB, Eurocard/Access, American Express, Diners ❖ Rooms: double 355 F, buffet breakfast 38 F ❖ Menus: 140 F, 200 F, 300 F, menu enfant 60 F ❖ à la carte: about 250 F ❖ Street parking in front of the hotel ❖ English spoken ❖ L S H B

RESTAURANT

La Grillade

16, rue de Reims
tel.: 26 55 44 22
fax: 26 54 01 74

Claude and Blanche Kindler run a welcoming and basically simple restaurant serving both fish and meats cooked to perfection over a wood fire. Meals are served outdoors in a pleasantly shaded terrace when the weather is fine.

Closed Sat. midday, Sun.; two weeks in Sept. ❖ Credit cards: Visa/CB, Eurocard/Access ❖ Menus: 78 F, 98 F, 165 F ❖ à la carte: about 130 F ❖ English spoken

51460 L'EPINE (MARNE)
Calais 336 km – Reims 54 km – Chalons-sur-Marne 9 km

HOTEL-RESTAURANT

**Hôtel-Restaurant
Aux Armes de
Champagne**
31, avenue du
Luxembourg
tel.: 26 69 30 30
fax: 26 66 92 31

The dining room of this stylish hotel-restaurant overlooks the splendid, sixteenth-century cathedral of Notre-Dame de l'Epine, a magnificent, flamboyant, Gothic church which rather incongruously dominates this otherwise small and quiet Champagne village. The old coaching inn has been transformed by Denise and Jean-Paul Pérardel into one of the region's most comfortable halting places. There are thirty-seven bedrooms, all recently refurbished and luxuriously appointed; each has private bath or shower, w.c., television and telephone, and enjoy views either of the town square and cathedral or the pleasant and quiet gardens.

The main reason for coming here, though, is to enjoy the exceptional cuisine of young chef Patrick Michelon, wholly modern and innovative, yet firmly steeped in the traditions of the region. *Sous-presse de lapereau cuite au vin de Chardonnay*, for example, is a stylishly elegant and light *terrine* of rabbit served in a Chardonnay aspic together with the grilled rabbit liver and a fresh salad. Other specialities include *matelote des bords de Marne braisée au Champagne maderisé*, a hearty freshwater fish stew made with perch, pike, eels and frogs' legs; and superlative wild duck simply roasted and served with fresh figs.

Closed Sun. evening, Mon. Nov.–March; 9 Jan.–15 Feb. ❖ Credit cards: Visa/CB, Eurocard/Access ❖ Rooms: double 450–780 F, breakfast 60 F ❖ Menus: 110 F (lunch weekdays only), 210 F, 290 F, 480 F, menu enfant 100 F ❖ à la carte: about 350–450 F ❖ English spoken

51160 FONTAINE-SUR-AŸ (MARNE)
Calais 320 km – Epernay 14 km – Aÿ 8 km

CHAMBRE D'HÔTE

Au Beau Sarrazin
8, allée des Seigneurs
tel.: 26 52 30 25
fax: 26 52 03 99

This quiet farm in the high country above Aÿ where wheat is cultivated in place of vines makes a peaceful base from which to explore the Champagne region. Here, the Lutun family offer both *chambres d'hôte* as well as a *gîte* that is available either for the weekend or the week. There is one bedroom in the large, typical, *champenois* farmhouse itself, a comfortable, traditional *chambre* with its own private bathroom and w.c.; there is also an adjoining room with two single beds which can be used by families. Alternatively, there are four atmospheric and individually decorated *chambres* in the adjoining *grenier*, each of which has its own shower room and w.c. These are available as separate *chambres* during the week, but on weekends they are rented out as a *gîte* that sleeps up to nine, and includes a downstairs kitchenette and huge sitting room with an old, wooden fireplace and long trestle table.

Rooms: two persons 220–250 F including breakfast ❖ gîte weekend (Fri. evening–Sun. afternoon) 1300 F

51160 GERMAINE (MARNE)
Calais 302 km – Epernay 15 km – Reims 20 km

FERME AUBERGE

La Ferme Auberge des Bœufs
tel.: 26 52 88 25
fax: 26 52 84 08

While Champagne has no shortage of fine if pricey restaurants specializing in an elegant *haute cuisine champenoise*, it is particularly satisfying to find such a warm and genuine farmhouse restaurant like this one, personally run by Isabelle and Bernard Verdonk on their working farm in the heart of the densely wooded Parc Naturel Régional de la Montagne de Reims. This was the first *ferme auberge* in the *département* of the Marne and has been in operation since 1981. Here, on weekends only and by reservation, the Verdonks serve filling and hearty set meals utilizing their own seasonal produce as well as that from neighbouring farms. While Bernard provides a warm welcome to guests, Isabelle herself does the cooking, based on traditional and family recipes; specialities include *pain de la reine, tourte champenoise, poulet au marc de Champagne, filet de porc au ratafia, jambon braisé* and homemade *tartes* and *gâteaux*. The 100 F menu always offers a choice of first course, then main course with garden vegetables, salad, local cheeses and dessert. House Champagne costs 130 F.

Open Sat. midday and evening, Sun. midday from 15 April–25 Oct. Essential to reserve. Groups other times by reservation ❖ Menu: 100 F, menu enfant 50 F

51700 IGNY COMBLIZY (MARNE)

Calais 331 km – Epernay 25 km – Dormans 10 km

CHAMBRE D'HÔTE
AND *TABLE D'HÔTE*

**Château du Ru
Jacquier**
D18
tel.: 26 57 10 84
fax: 26 57 11 85

Monsieur and Madame Robert Granger are proprietors of a beautiful, eighteenth-century château surrounded by 15 hectares of gardens and park in the Vallée de la Marne 15 kilometres south of the A4 *autoroute* (exit Dormans). They offer six lovely *chambres* on the second and third floors, each with private bathroom and w.c.

The dining room where they serve *table d'hôte* meals is beautifully furnished, and the simple, classic meals are accompanied by local Champagnes.

Open all year. Reservations advisable ❖ Rooms: two persons 350–450 F including breakfast ❖ Table d'hôte: from 150 F

51490 MONTCHENOT (MARNE)

Calais 293 km – Epernay 17 km – Reims 11 km

RESTAURANT

Le Grand Cerf
50, route Nationale
tel.: 26 97 60 07
fax: 26 97 64 24

The most direct road between Reims and Epernay is the route Nationale. This nineteenth-century restaurant makes a pleasant stop along the way. It is a sophisticated country inn where the people of the city go on weekends and where wine growers and Champagne *négociants* entertain their clients. Patron Alain Guichaoua comes from Brittany which probably explains why seafoods feature heavily: *soupe de moules à l'estragon, crème de chou-fleur aux crustacés, salade tiède de St-Jacques au foie gras chaud, panaché de poissons aux algues et baies roses*. Chef Dominique Giraudeau also prepares classic cuisine with a strong, regional accent: *oreille de porc grillée au jus de viande, civet de lapin fermier, filet de bœuf à la moëlle et au Bouzy*. The menus change with the seasons and the Champagne list is extensive and reasonably priced.

Closed Wed., Sun. evening ❖ Credit cards: Eurocard/Access, American Express ❖ Menus: 175 F (weekdays only), 250 F, 350 F, 420 F, menu enfant 120 F ❖ à la carte: about 350–400 F ❖ English and German spoken

51160 MUTIGNY (MARNE)

Calais 312 km – Epernay 9 km – Reims 30 km

CHAMBRE D'HÔTE
AND TABLE D'HÔTE

**Manoir de
Montflambert**

tel.: 26 52 33 21

This seventeenth-century manor house located on the border of the forest of the Parc Naturel Régional de la Montagne de Reims is a retreat of great charm and repose. Madame Renée Rampacek has six superior *chambres* all individually decorated with period furniture and each has private bathroom and w.c. The grounds are lovely and the house could serve as a base for walking in the forest or for visiting vineyards. Three-course evening meals are served during the week by reservation, while Madame Rampacek serves a special *menu gastronomique* on Saturday evenings.

Open all year ❖ Credit cards: Visa/CB, Eurocard/Access ❖ Rooms: two persons 350 F, 450 F, 600 F including breakfast ❖ Table d'hôte: 170 F (weekdays), 210 F (Saturday)

51100 REIMS (MARNE) 🛒

Marché   Daily except Sun.
Calais 280 km – Epernay 26 km – Paris 144 km

HOTEL-RESTAURANT

Boyer Les Crayères
64, boulevard
H. Vasnier
tel.: 26 82 80 80
fax: 26 82 65 52

How remarkable that just ten minutes from the busy centre of Reims lies this quiet and beautiful, nineteenth-century château in its own 7 hectares of wooded grounds, a fitting and grand home for one of the great restaurants of France. Les Crayères was originally conceived and designed under the watchful eye of Madame Louise Pommery, one of Champagne's formidable *grandes dames*. Today, it is the home of Gérard and Elyane Boyer whose famous Les Crayères restaurant has earned no less than three rosettes from Michelin and nineteen points and four toques from Gault-Millau. This is a luxury establishment in every sense, the elegant, period furniture, the paintings and the formal dining rooms matched only by the brilliance of Boyer's individual *haute cuisine champenoise* – classic and in touch with its essential roots, yet quietly innovative at the same time, as in *pied de porc farci au foie gras et aux cèpes*, a magnificently elegant version of a basically rustic dish! Naturally, Boyer utilizes only the finest and freshest ingredients – particularly fine fish and shellfish from Brittany and Normandy, freshwater fish such as *sandre* and *brochet*, game from the forests of the Ardennes in season, a magnificent selection of primarily local and regional cheeses. His desserts are not only exquisitely delicious, they are visual works of art. The wine *carte* lists just about every *grande marque* Champagne plus an enviable range of mainly classic wines of Burgundy and Bordeaux.

The hotel is part of the Relais & Château group of luxury hotels. The sixteen rooms in the château itself, as well as the suite and duplexes located in the pavilion in the grounds, are magnificently fitted, all furnished and decorated individually in period style, with all the luxuries you would expect of a hotel of this class.

Closed Mon., Tue. midday ❖ Credit cards: Visa/CB, Eurocard/Access, American Express ❖ Rooms: 990–1590 F, breakfast 90 F ❖ à la carte: about 500–750 F ❖ Parking ❖ English spoken

Reims cathedral

HOTEL

Hôtel Crystal
86, place Drouet d'Erlon
tel.: 26 88 44 44
fax: 26 47 49 28

The 2-star Crystal is our favourite small hotel in Reims, located along the town's main drag but set back from the road overlooking quiet gardens and a central, interior courtyard. There are thirty-one rooms which you reach by way of an old-fashioned but functional caged-in lift; the rooms, all furnished differently, have either a private shower or bath, w.c., television, telephone and mini-bar. They are comfortable and clean if somewhat dated.

Rooms: double 260–330 F, breakfast 29 F ❖ Underground parking nearby

Small Hotels and Restaurants

HOTEL-RESTAURANT

**Hôtel-Gril
Campanile**
avenue Georges
Pompidou
Val de Murigny II
tel.: 26 36 66 94
fax: 26 49 95 40

If you are driving along the A4 *autoroute* and can't face going into the city centre, this 2-star chain motel is a useful stop. There are sixty rooms, each with private bath and w.c., television and telephone and a pleasant garden where meals are served in summer.

It is located to the south of the city just 1.5 kilometres from the A4 *autoroute* (exit St-Rémi Murigny).

Open all year ❖ Credit cards: Visa/CB, Eurocard/Access, American Express ❖ Rooms: double 278 F, breakfast 29 F ❖ Menus: 80 F, 83 F, 102 F, menu enfant 39 F ❖ Parking ❖ English and German spoken

---

RESTAURANT

Le Vigneron
place Paul Jamot
tel.: 26 47 00 71
fax: 26 47 87 66

We first met Hervé Liégent more than a dozen years ago when he had ambitiously just set out to create a true *champenois* restaurant in the region's capital, serving not *haute cuisine* but rather the authentic foods of the region as eaten by the *vignerons* themselves, including such simple but satisfying dishes as *salade aux lardons* and *andouillette de Troyes*.

The restaurant has since expanded and today it is a well-established, city-centre favourite, located not far from the cathedral, its rustic but stylish dining room full of wine paraphanalia, Champagne posters and a small museum of wine makers' implements, tools and barrels.

Over the years, the cooking at Le Vigneron has similarly evolved and, while maintaining its country roots, it is now much more considered in its preparation, and stylish in presentation. But this is still the place to come to taste the true foods

Le Vigneron, Reims

of the region: *terrine de lapin en gelée, le brochet de la Marne beurre champenoise, le sandre poché aux choux et oignons frits, le canard au ratafia de Champagne*. There is a superlative cheeseboard made up exclusively with local and regional cheeses, and a meal is best concluded with a cleansing, if powerful, *sorbet au marc de Champagne et ses raisins*. The restaurant boasts an exceptional Champagne list (there are over 150 examples) as well as a comprehensive selection of still Coteaux Champenois and Rosé des Riceys wines.

Closed Sat. midday, Sun.; first fortnight in Aug.; 23 Dec.–2 Jan. ❖ Credit cards: Visa/CB, Eurocard/Access ❖ Menu: 155 F ❖ à la carte: about 250 F

RESTAURANT-
BOUTIQUE

**La Table en
Périgord**
47, place Drouet
d'Erlon
tel.: 26 47 73 74

Monsieur Alain Ebrard runs this friendly shop-cum-restaurant specializing in fine produce and products of his native Périgord: *foie gras de canard et d'oie, confits, cassoulet, magret de canard* and a good selection of wines from the southwest. You can come here simply for a *dégustation* of *foie gras*, for a *salade composée*, or for good, two-course menus utilizing the Pierre Champion products on sale in the shop. The 95 F menu offers a choice of *terrine périgourdine au foie de canard* or *salade aux gésiers confits et magret fumé*, followed by *magret de canard sauce aux cèpes* or *tourte au confit de canard aux trois légumes*. Meals finish with a selection of desserts and ice creams from the southwest.

Closed Sun., one week in Feb., three weeks in July ❖ Credit cards: Visa/CB, Eurocard/Access ❖ Menus: 74 F, 95 F, 126 F ❖ à la carte: about 150 F
❖ English spoken

51390 ROSNAY (MARNE)
Calais 294 km – Reims 12 km – A4 autoroute (exit Reims-Tinqueux) 8 km

---

CHAMBRE D'HÔTE

**Domaine des
Oiseaux**
12, Grande Rue
tel.: 26 03 63 07

Madame Jeannine Legros's pretty home in a typical village just ten minutes outside Reims is located on the fringe of the Champagne vineyards and makes an excellent base for visiting Reims and touring the wine country. This rambling house with lovely gardens and a small swimming pool is a cool respite from the city heat in summer: indeed, it is something of a rural oasis, the garden full of birds including

*Domaine des
Oiseaux, Rosnay*

Madame Legros's two garrulous parrots, Victor and Aglaée.
There are five comfortable and individually decorated
chambres, four of which have private bath and w.c. One of
the rooms has a small balcony overlooking the gardens.
Guests can enjoy the large sitting room, sitting around *au
coin du feu* together with Madame Legros in winter.

Madame Legros can advise you on visiting local
Champagne growers, and she sells gift hampers stocked
with quality *produits du terroir* including Champagne, *confit
de canard*, *terrine de lapin*, *confiture*, *miel* and other local
specialities: just what is needed for a *pique-nique* in the
vineyards or an impromptu meal in your room.

Open all year ❖ Rooms: two persons 260–280 F including breakfast

51400 SEPT-SAULX (MARNE)

Calais 305 km – Reims 23 km – Chalons-sur-Marne 28 km

HOTEL-RESTAURANT

Hôtel-Restaurant
Le Cheval Blanc
rue du Moulin
tel.: 26 03 90 27
fax: 26 03 97 09

The Robert family has been installed in this *ancien relais de la poste* for no less than five generations. Today, this delightful country hotel, surrounded by its own gardens and parkland through which flows the River Vesle, is a *relais du silence* that is indeed a quiet and peaceful retreat. The hotel offers twenty comfortable rooms, each with its own bathroom, w.c., television, telephone and mini-bar, and five superior suites. The restaurant, under the direction of Monsieur Bernard Robert, serves classic cuisine – *coquilles St-Jacques et langoustines au sabayon de Champagne, soufflé de foie gras, emincé de bœuf et son jus de truffe* – accompanied by a superlative list of Champagnes plus a better than average list of wines from the classic regions of France.

Closed 15 Jan.–15 Feb. ❖ Credit cards: Visa/CB, Eurocard/Access, American Express, Diners ❖ Rooms: double 450 F, suite 700–980 F, breakfast 50 F ❖ Menus: 150 F (lunch only except Sun.), 190 F, 290 F, 380 F ❖ à la carte: about 300–350 F ❖ English spoken

51530 VINAY (MARNE)

Calais 312 km – Epernay 6 km

HOTEL-RESTAURANT

Hostellerie La
Briqueterie
4, route de Sézanne
tel.: 26 59 99 99
fax: 26 59 92 10

This extremely stylish hotel-restaurant is located just south of Epernay at the foot of the prestigious Côte des Blancs vineyards. Set in its own 4-hectare park, it is a place of great charm and quiet repose. There are forty rooms and two suites, all individually furnished and luxuriously equipped, a heated, indoor swimming pool, two saunas and an exercise room. This certainly would make a lovely and restful, luxury weekend break amidst the wine country of Champagne.

The restaurant of La Briqueterie is well known and highly renowned for its elegant *haute cuisine champenoise*, served in the warm, atmospheric, beamed dining room. Chef Lieven Vercouteren naturally offers those refined, luxury foods which diners have come to expect in restaurants of this quality – *foie gras d'oie au ratafia de Champagne, nage glacée de homard au consommé d'étrilles, turbot poché au sabayon de Champagne –*

while he has also researched traditional foods of the region and presents them in a lighter and more elegant manner: *potée champenoise, pieds de porc farcis au ris de veau, tournedos poêlé au Bouzy*. Simpler lunches are served in the less formal patio dining room.

Closed 23–28 Dec. ❖ Credit cards: Visa/CB, Eurocard/Access, American Express, Diners ❖ Rooms: double 710–845 F, buffet breakfast on the patio 70 F ❖ Menus: 170 F (lunch served on the patio), 230 F (lunch), 335 F, 380 F ❖ à la carte: about 250–350 F ❖ English, German, Dutch and Italian spoken

UPPER NORMANDY

Upper Normandy, straddling the Seine valley across the *départements* of Seine-Maritime and Eure, lies at the extremity of the area covered by this volume. Rouen, the capital, can now be reached in under four hours from Calais. When the new dual carriageway via Abbeville is completed in 1996–97 this could be more than halved. Upper Normandy is a region that is accessible for a break as short as one or two nights, and there are compelling arguments for choosing to come here.

The great basin of the sinuous Seine extends across a landscape which, though densely wooded in parts, remains essentially open and

Rouen

wide, a marked contrast to the rest of Normandy with its more claustrophobic, rolling countryside, its farms and fields punctuated by hedges and herds of brown and white cows. Upper Normandy may be less well known and less overtly postcard pretty than its lower counterpart but it has its own charms and beauty. The so-called 'alabaster coast', with its impressive, flying buttress cliffs at Etretat, its great, sweeping beaches and its important fishing towns like Fécamp and Dieppe, certainly deserves to be visited. Even in mid-summer, its resorts are surprisingly accessible mid-week: but on weekends throughout the year, beware, as the proximity to Paris means that virtually the entire capital, or so it seems, can descend here *en masse*.

Inland, though, is another, quieter world. The Pays de Caux hinterland behind Fécamp and Etretat is rural France *par excellence*, while the Pays de Bray east of Rouen, south of Dieppe, is perhaps more typical of what most of us consider Normandy to be like: a land of apple orchards, half-timbered farmhouses, and rich, lush dairy land. Nearby lie the dense beech forests of Eawy and Lyons, while straddling the Seine lies the great Fôret de Brotonne, a Parc Naturel Régional made up of extensive woodland and protected countryside encompassing such historic and charming towns and villages as Pont-Audemer and Le Bec-Hellouin.

The Seine itself with its huge, snake-like, enclosed bends is indeed one of the great attractions of the region. It is not all that easy, or necessarily desirable, to follow the river in its entirety but, nonetheless, a journey through some of its principal attractions is more than satisfying: starting in Giverny with a visit to Monet's house and gardens, then continuing down river through Les Andelys with its magnificent, ruined castle of Richard the Lionheart, through mighty Rouen and up to typical river villages like Duclair and Caudebec-en-Caux, stopping en route to visit the abbey ruins of Jumièges, before eventually arriving where the river mouth widens towards Honfleur and Le Havre.

Rouen, the capital of Upper Normandy, certainly deserves more than a fleeting visit. The modern city sprawls across both sides of the river, and its vast, industrial suburbs extend well down the Seine valley. Rouen, though an inland city, is the fifth largest port in France. But the historic, medieval heart of the town is compact, easily visited and hugely atmospheric. There is the great, Gothic cathedral which we all feel we know from the series of paintings by Monet. The narrow streets are lined with tall, medieval, half-timbered buildings. And Rouen, of course, is inextricably associated with Jeanne d'Arc. It was here that the maiden warrior was tried by the English, later

Hôtel Belle-Isle-sur-Risle, Pont-Audemer

to be burned at the stake in the Place du Vieux Marché.

Whether in simple, country *auberges*, welcoming *chambres d'hôte*, really fine and luxurious small hotels for a special break, half-timbered, Norman inns or great, city-centre restaurants, the always ample, always satisfying cuisine of Normandy is one of the most rewarding reasons for visiting the region.

à Table

Normandy is a region which yields unstintingly and generously an abundance of good things to eat and drink: superb fish and shellfish from the coast; duck, pork and good *charcuterie*; a profusion of excellent fruit and vegetables; rich dairy products such as sweet, unsalted, Norman butter, tangy *crème fraîche* and a profusion of excellent cheeses; and farmhouse *cîdre* and calvados.

Norman cuisine is characterized, above all, by its ample use of cream, butter, apples and calvados. Pork, chicken or fish such as turbot are cooked in cider and apples *à la Vallée d'Auge*. Mussels are served *à la crème*. *Sole à la dieppoise* is Dover sole cooked in cider, the sauce thickened with butter and cream, sometimes garnished with mussels and shrimps. Tripe is *flambéed* and simmered slowly in calvados, the sauce eventually finished with – what else – cream. Norman cuisine is nothing if not ample: these are rich, satisfying and filling foods, definitely not recommended for those on a diet – but which French, regional cuisine is? The Normans

themselves are great trenchermen; thus, we imagine, developed the custom of the *trou normand*, a tot of fiery calvados taken mid-meal in order to create 'a hole' in the stomach to aid and quicken digestion, enabling you to eat even more.

After the main course, a profusion of fine but, of course, creamy and rich, Norman cheeses inevitably follows. Camembert is the most famous of all French cheeses, known and enjoyed throughout the world, but the real thing when it is just right, as usually encountered here – farm-produced from unpasteurized *lait cru*, aged precisely to perfect maturity so that it is soft but not overly runny – is well worth all the fuss. Mild but assertive Pont l'Evêque, and the richer, more pungent, rind-washed Livarot are two more great and ancient cheeses, while Neufchâtel, from the Pays de Bray, has

Crème fraîche, Dieppe market

been produced in that region since the eleventh century. A relative newcomer which demonstrates the Norman penchant for the rich and super-rich is Brillat-Savarin, made not from double cream but from full triple cream with an absurdly high fat content.

If, at its most basic, we find that for our tastes Norman cuisine does have a tendency to gild gold, fortunately, as elsewhere throughout northern France, a new breed of the best chefs in scores of fine restaurants throughout the region take the essentially superb ingredients of both sea and land, and, while respecting Norman traditions, present them in lighter, more elegant and refined ways. Even the *trou normand* can translate into a delicate and refreshing *sorbet* of apple and calvados served between courses.

LE MENU DU TERROIR

moules à la crème
foie gras normande de canard
pieds de mouton farcis à la rouennaise

gratin de coquilles St-Jacques
sole à la normande
la marmite dieppoise

canard à la rouennaise
poulet vallée d'auge
tripes à la mode de Caen

Camembert fermier
Livarot
Pont l'Evêque
Neufchâtel
Brillat-Savarin

sorbet au calvados
tarte aux pommes normande
tarte tatin
mirlitons

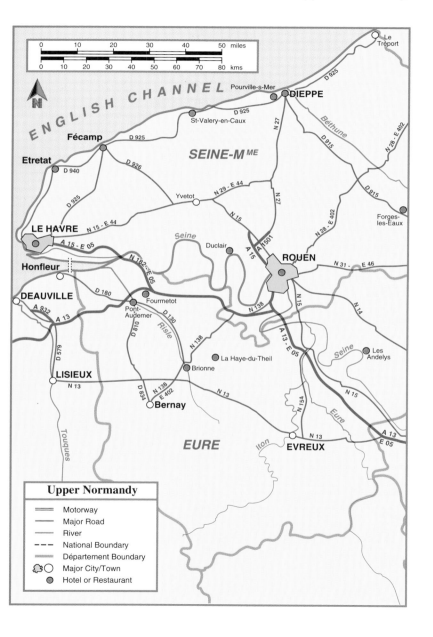

Upper Normandy

▬▬▬	Motorway
———	Major Road
———	River
– – –	National Boundary
▬▬▬	Département Boundary
⬡○	Major City/Town
●	Hotel or Restaurant

27700 LES ANDELYS (EURE)
Marché Mon.
Calais 256 km – Rouen 38 km – Paris 93 km

HOTEL-RESTAURANT

**Hôtel-Restaurant
La Chaîne d'Or**
27, rue Grande
tel.: 32 54 00 31
fax: 32 54 05 68

This famous, eighteenth-century inn is located on the banks of the Seine below the ruins of Richard the Lionheart's favourite castle, Château Gaillard. The Chaîne d'Or itself, several centuries later, served as a toll house from which a chain was strung across the river to an island. This could be drawn tight to prevent boats from travelling up or down river unless they paid the requisite fee. So lucrative was this levy that the barrier became known as the *chaîne d'or*, hence the name of the inn.

In recent years, Monique and Jean-Claude Foucault have considerably upgraded this old favourite stopping place. The ten bedrooms are characterful with modern comforts including private bath or shower, w.c., telephone, television, mini-bar and soundproofing to keep out the noise of the river barges which can be surprisingly active during the night.

The restaurant is now one of the top establishments in the Seine valley. Certainly it is one of the most pleasant, the pretty, pink dining room enjoying wonderful views of the river in all its activity. The cuisine, under the direction of chef Francis Chevalliez, has gained a considerable reputation for a classical, neo-classical and regional repertoire.

Closed Sun. evening, Mon.; Jan. ❖ Credit cards: Visa/CB, Eurocard/Access, American Express ❖ Rooms: double 395–560 F, breakfast 48 F ❖ Menus: 135 F, 180 F, 220 F, 280 F ❖ à la carte: 300–400 F

27800 BRIONNE (EURE)
Marché Thur., Sun.
Calais 259 km – Rouen 41 km – Pont-Audemer 26 km

CHAMBRE D'HÔTE

Le Cœur de Lion
14, boulevard de la
République
tel.: 32 43 40 35

Peter Baker, a retired RAF pilot, and his wife Hazel emigrated to France in 1988 and since then have been renting out *chambres* in their large, nineteenth-century, Norman house on the outskirts of Brionne. There are seven rooms available, four of which are large doubles with full en suite, private facilities. The other three rooms are smaller and each has a shower and basin but share a w.c. in the hall. The rooms are pleasant and clean and enjoy peaceful views over the gardens or across to the nearby *base de loisirs*, a municipal lake with facilities for canoeing and sailing, with a beach, children's play area, water slide, mini-golf and picnic sites.

Most of the guests, including the French who now make up about half the clientèle, stop to enjoy Hazel's *table d'hôte*

evening meals. Everyone sits together at a large table and Hazel serves a four-course, traditional French meal which includes a choice of starter, meat or fish main course – *escalope de dinde Normande*, *truite aux amandes* – followed by local cheeses and a homemade dessert. House wine costs 38 F a bottle.

Closed 15 Dec.–15 Jan. ❖ Credit cards: Visa/CB, Eurocard/Access ❖ Rooms: two persons 175– 215 F, three persons 270 F including breakfast ❖ Table d'hôte: 85 F ❖ English spoken

Peter and Hazel Baker, Brionne

76200 DIEPPE (SEINE-MARITIME)

Marché   Tue., Thur., Sat.
Calais 175 km – Rouen 60 km – Le Havre 105 km

HOTEL

Hôtel Aguado
30, boulevard de Verdun
tel.: 35 84 27 00
fax: 35 06 17 61

We dare say that when this 3-star hotel was built in 1957 it was probably the bee's knees of Dieppe. Today, with its exterior façade decorated with happy beach scenes and its neon sign spanning the road that leads to the beach, with its chrome-fronted dressers and curvaceous, fake leather settees in the rooms, it appears to us so charmingly out of date that it is almost, although not quite, a 'modern' period piece.

This always welcoming hotel, personally run by Alain Bert for more than twenty years, remains one of our favourites in Dieppe, primarily for its outstanding position overlooking the sea, just behind the principal areas for restaurants and shopping. It is essential, we think, to request and pay extra for one of the many rooms with sea views; they are spacious and comfortable and have all the necessary facilities, including bath or shower, w.c., hair dryer, television, telephone and mini-bar. We love to watch the busy seafront and the sea in the early evening and enjoy gazing at the long line of lights that stretches from harbour to cliff. The best time to stay here is Friday night in order to enjoy Dieppe's superlative and immense Saturday market which sprawls out on the main shopping area just behind the hotel.

Open all year ❖ Credit cards: Visa/CB, Eurocard/Access, American Express, Diners ❖ Rooms: 320–425 F, breakfast 38 F ❖ Street parking in front of the hotel ❖ English spoken

---

HOTEL

Hôtel Epsom
11, boulevard de
Verdun
tel.: 35 84 10 18
fax: 35 40 03 00

The Epsom is a small, moderately priced hotel located on the Dieppe seafront and has twenty-eight plainly furnished but pleasant rooms: wood-panelled bathrooms, brown, hessian walls, simple furnishings. The majority have outstanding sea views while the others offer an interesting prospect of the old roofs of the town; each room has a private bath or shower, w.c., television and telephone.

There is no restaurant but downstairs there is a large, popular cocktail bar decorated with equestrian themes where the piano is played at weekends. This bar is apparently highly popular not only with hotel guests but with locals and Parisians alike who come especially at weekends. Max Gréboval, the young and enthusiastic owner of the hotel, is a member of the

*Hôtel Epsom,
Dieppe*

Confrerie du Sabre d'Or, so anyone who cares to purchase a bottle of house Champagne and open it by slashing off the neck of the bottle with a sword can happily do so. Max will show you how to do it safely and ensure that you receive a certificate from the *Confrerie* for your efforts.

Open all year ❖ Credit cards: Visa/CB, Eurocard/Access, American Express, Diners ❖ Rooms: double 265–295 F, breakfast 30 F ❖ Limited parking in front of the hotel as well as street parking ❖ English spoken

---

HOTEL-RESTAURANT

Au Grand Duquesne

15, place St-Jacques
tel.: 35 84 21 51
fax: 35 84 29 83

The Grand Duquesne, centrally located in the heart of Dieppe's shopping area near the Place St-Jacques, is probably better known as a restaurant than a hotel, but it is a useful and more than pleasant find on both counts. Certainly the Hobbé family who have owned and run it for the last eight years have made considerable efforts to please both their local and foreign clientèle, and the restaurant is rightly popular. The dining room is prettily decorated but not formal and the Hobbés offer a range of mainly seafood oriented menus of exceptional value that have proved to be very popular. The least expensive, for example, is quite adequate and includes *moules à la crème*, followed by fish such as skate or trout, with a choice of either salad and cheese or homemade dessert. As the menus rise in price, there is more choice but the dishes are not overly complicated and remain primarily home-cooked, traditional foods utilizing local and seasonal produce. All the breads and *pâtisseries* are baked on the premises.

There are twelve small but newly renovated and comfortable rooms, nine of which have full private facilities, television and telephone. In spite of the hotel's location in the heart of the town, the bedrooms are quiet and calm. A disadvantage, however, is that there is no private parking, so perhaps the Duquesne would be more suitable for visitors without their own transport.

Credit cards: Visa/CB, Eurocard/Access, American Express, Diners ❖ Rooms: double 160–250 F ❖ Menus: 69 F, 105 F, 139 F, 189 F, menu enfant 50 F ❖ English spoken

Small Hotels and Restaurants

RESTAURANT

La Marmite Dieppoise
8, rue St-Jean
tel.: 35 84 24 26

An old Dieppoise favourite, this traditional, family restaurant just a block back from the seafront remains popular with locals and visitors alike for the copious and well-prepared plates of fish and shellfish served in a pretty, family-style dining room. Chef Jean-Pierre Toussat has a deft and precise touch in the preparation of such dishes as *bar grillé au beurre blanc d'estragon* and *turbot au chou et basilac* but the undoubted star of the restaurant is the famous local speciality for which it is named. The *marmite dieppoise*, as served here, really is a regional dish worth trying, a sort of soupy-stew made with fish such as *barbue*, *lotte*, *julienne* and *sole* as well as *moules* and *langoustines*, poached in a concentrated fish stock, then finished in a sauce made from the stock together with *crème fraîche* and other seasonings. It is an abundant dish indeed, served in a white, ceramic chafing dish which sits over a spirit burner which keeps the whole bubbling mixture piping hot: a fine communal pot to dip into and thus an excellent centrepiece for a special lunch.

Closed Thur. evening except July and Aug., Sun. evening, Mon.; end of June to early July; early Jan. ❖ Credit card: Visa/CB ❖ Menus: 80 F (weekdays lunch only), 135 F, 200 F ❖ à la carte: about 200 F

RESTAURANT

La Mélie
2 et 4, Grande-Rue du Pollet
tel.: 35 84 21 19

Walk over the Colbert bridge, away from the hoardes of day-trippers who overrun the town when the ferry docks, to the quieter, more charming fishermen's quarter on the far side of the harbour known as Le Pollet where many of Dieppe's fisherfolk still live today. This stylish fish restaurant at the far end is considered by locals to be one of the best in town. Certainly chef Guy Brachais does not have to go far to find the freshest fish and shellfish: nor for that matter do any of Dieppe's restaurateurs, though few are able to handle their ingredients with more delicacy, finesse and respect to allow the fresh flavours of the sea to shine through. The *marmite polletaise* is a full meal in itself, comprising the liquid in which the fish has been gently poached, finished and served first as a flavoursome, concentrated soup, followed by the fish and shellfish.

Dieppe harbour

Closed Sun. evening, Mon. ❖ Credit cards: Visa/CB, Eurocard/Access, American Express, Diners ❖ Menus: 170 F, 238 F (including wine) ❖ à la carte: about 250–300 F

RESTAURANT

Restaurant du Port
99, quai Henri IV
tel.: 35 84 36 64

Dieppe's *quai* will inevitably change in character when the ferry port is moved in 1994 to the other side of the harbour entrance. There will be less traffic and vehicles will be able to exit the town far more easily than is now the case. The line of restaurants opposite where the boats presently disembark will no doubt continue to do well all the same, and diners at the pavement tables will no longer fear that a juggernaut will run over their toes.

The Port is towards the far end of restaurants that stretch down from the town centre, but make your way to this small, typical favourite all the same. Madame Mouny gives a warm and genuinely friendly welcome while husband and chef Michel continues to serve simple but excellent fish menus. They have been here for the past eighteen years and have built up a faithful clientèle who return again and again to enjoy basically simple foods which are most remarkable for freshness, quality and presentation. The 80 F menu, for example, offers either *moules*, a copious *assiette des fruits de mer* or homemade *soupe de poissons*, followed by fried whiting or a *gratin* of sweet

Dieppe scallops served with fresh *haricots verts*. This is the sort of fun, unpretentious and inexpensive restaurant which we all cross the Channel to find.

Closed Thur. except May–Sept.
❖ Credit cards: Visa/CB, Eurocard/Access, American Express, Diners
❖ Menus: 80 F, 90 F, 145 F, 180 F
❖ à la carte: about 150 F

Restaurant du Port, Dieppe

76480 DUCLAIR (SEINE-MARITIME)
Marché   Tue.
Calais 257 km – Rouen 19 km – Dieppe 59 km

HOTEL-RESTAURANT

Hôtel de la Poste
286, quai de la Libération
tel.: 35 37 50 04

Located on the town *quai* virtually opposite where the *bac* trundles across the Seine, this otherwise unremarkable, 2-star *Logis de France* is credited with the creation of one of the most famous dishes of Normandy, *canard à la rouennaise*. This dish, great delicacy though it is, demonstrates the French at their most ingeniously gruesome. The Duclair duck that is said to be half wild, half domestic, must be despatched by suffocation so that it can be cooked without loss of blood, a process greatly appreciated by *gourmands* for the rich and gamey flavour this imparts to the flesh. After the duck has been roasted, the meat is carved off and the carcass is put into a silver press to extract the remaining juices for a sauce made with red wine and cognac mixed with a purée of the duck heart and liver.

How did such a dish ever come to be devised, you may well ask. Duclair and neighbouring Yvetot have long been centres for the *élevage* of the specially bred Duclair duck. As the live ducks were transported by ferry across the river, the locals conjecture that a number of birds ended up suffocating in the crush. The French being, well, the French, an enterprising farmer began to sell the 'boat kill' as *canards au sang* and they soon came to be considered a local delicacy. Monsieur Henri Denise, the great-grandfather of Eric Monthier, the current owner of the Hôtel de la Poste, subsequently devised the famous recipe which, with considerable leeway and variation, can be found throughout the region today.

This is still the place to come, therefore, to eat Duclair duck at the source, as it were, in the hotel's first-floor dining room which enjoys outstanding views of the river in all its activity. The speciality, here called *canard à la Denise*, is prepared to order, so if you are sure that you want to try it, you should telephone in advance, especially at weekends, just to make sure it is available. The restaurant also serves good, traditional, if unremarkable, Norman cuisine.

The hotel also has nineteen rooms, most of which have their own private shower or bath, w.c., television and telephone. They are clean and strictly functional but no matter: an endless stream of entertainment is provided by the great barges and boats plying France's mightiest river.

Open all year. Restaurant closed Sun. evening, Mon. ❖ Credit cards: Visa/CB, Eurocard/Access, American Express, Diners ❖ Rooms: double 190–240 F, breakfast 25 F ❖ Menus: 75 F, 125 F, 175 F ❖ à la carte: about 150–200 F

76790 ETRETAT (SEINE-MARITIME)

Calais 243 km – Le Havre 28 km – Fécamp 16 km

HOTEL-RESTAURANT

**Hôtel-Restaurant
Le Donjon**
Chemin de Saint Clair
tel.: 35 27 08 23
fax: 35 29 92 24

Le Donjon is located just outside Etretat, literally raised several steps above the hullaballoo and crowds down below. Located in a curious, early nineteenth century château constructed in the shape of a medieval tower, it occupies an enviable position overlooking the *falaises* of Etretat, the beach and sea, and the bustling town below. This select and rather special hotel has just eight rooms, each highly individual and furnished and decorated in its own style. The sexiest is undoubtedly the *Orientale*, a large corner room with striking, deep mustard coloured carpet, black satin bedspread, orange curtains, and ceiling-high French windows opening on to a superb view of the cliffs; the bathroom is equally spacious and luxurious and has a jacuzzi. The other rooms, though not as opulent or as large, are as individual in their own ways. There is a comfortable *salon-bar* and in summer a decent-sized swimming pool.

Etretat

This is certainly a place to come for a special, romantic weekend.

The restaurant of Le Donjon is highly regarded, not just with guests but with locals and Parisians who come here all year round, especially at weekends. Madame Abo Dib, the owner, has stamped her inimitable if hardly subtle style on the dining room, too, which is decorated in a rather vivid, acid yellow which succeeds in distracting from the ever present cliff view. The cuisine, however, is not at all brash or overdone but is squarely classic with a strong emphasis on fresh fish, shellfish and duck;

specialities include *mouclade à la fleur de safran, gigot de lotte aux pleurottes* and *magret de canard aux trois sauces*.

Open all year ❖ Credit cards: Visa/CB, Eurocard/Access, American Express, Diners ❖ Rooms: demi-pension 600 F per person (800 F per person for *Orientale*) which includes dinner, bed and breakfast ❖ Menus: 160 F, 260 F ❖ à la carte: about 200–300 F ❖ English spoken

---

RESTAURANT

L'Huîtrière
Front de Mer
tel.: 35 27 02 82

There are so many restaurants vying for trade in Etretat that it can be hard to make an intelligent choice. However, it is not possible to go wrong at this simple restaurant which specializes, above all, in *fruits de mer*: the shellfish platters are fresh, well prepared, well presented and copious, and the restaurant's position along the seafront not far from the cliffs is superb. You can choose to eat upstairs in the first-floor dining room which has excellent panoramic views or you can eat downstairs and watch the chefs prepare the shellfish. There are a number of different *plateaux des fruits de mer* on offer, the most extravagant of which include whole lobsters and crabs. Meals conclude with excellent, homemade desserts, including a sensational *tarte tatin* best enjoyed straight from the oven.

Open daily except Mon. out of season ❖ Credit cards: Visa/CB, Eurocard/Access, American Express, Diners ❖ Menus: 95 F, 150 F, menus enfants 42 F, 60 F ❖ à la carte: *plateaux des fruits de mer* from 140 F (one person) to 530 F (three persons) ❖ English spoken

---

76400 FÉCAMP (SEINE-MARITIME) 🍴

Marché   Sat.
Calais 227 km – Le Havre 40 km – Dieppe 66 km

RESTAURANT

Le Viking
63, boulevard Albert
1er
tel.: 35 29 22 92
fax: 35 29 45 24

Come to this popular, seafront restaurant and view a microcosm of the social divisions of France. Two separate staircases lead to the dining rooms on the first floor, thus separating the hoi polloi from the élite: the staircase to the right leads to a very smart, nouvelle-inspired restaurant complete with all the trappings – enormous porcelain plates, linen napkins, large wine goblets, frosty head waiter; the staircase to the left leads to a more egalitarian, cheek by

Fécamp

jowl *brasserie* as well as to a *self* where workers, fishermen, truck drivers carry their trays for themselves. All three manifestations of the Viking enjoy the same superb view over the beaches and alabaster cliffs of Fécamp.

For the record, we initially started out up the right staircase, attracted by the restaurant's superb 90 F lunch time only menu which offered a fish *terrine* in a herb cream sauce, followed by *rosettes de limande sole sauce moules*. However, although we actually got as far as sitting down (fortunately did not start on the bread rolls), we found the atmosphere decidely *pas sympathique* so we left (the only people dining there were unsmiling salesmen and old couples with small dogs). So, down the stairs, then up the left hand staircase we went. The *brasserie*, unfortunately, was full so we actually ended up in the *self*. French cafeterias, on the whole, can be remarkably good, and this was no exception: we enjoyed an excellent 50 F menu with a choice of first courses, a main course of meat or fish, followed by cheese or dessert. As the man says, you pays your money, you takes your choice.

Closed Sun. evening out of season, Mon. ❖ Credit cards: Visa/CB, Eurocard/ Access ❖ Menus: restaurant 90 F (weekday lunch only), 155 F, 220 F, 275 F; brasserie 68 F; self 50 F ❖ à la carte: restaurant about 250–300 F

76440 FORGES-LES-EAUX (SEINE-MARITIME)
Marché Thur.
Calais 181 km – Rouen 42 km – Abbeville 68 km

RESTAURANT
WITH ROOMS

2 km S.E. at
Le Fossé

Auberge de Beau Lieu
D915
tel.: 35 90 50 36
fax: 35 90 35 98

Forges-les-Eaux is a rather curious, once popular, minor spa town in the heart of the Pays de Bray. Today, the town serves as something of a market centre for the surrounding country but the spa itself on the outskirts appears to have dried up. The *buvette* at the entrance to the park has apparently not functioned for over a year and there is now a neglected air to the place.

No matter: the best reason for coming here today is to visit Patrick Ramelet's small, roadside inn just outside town. Here, in a small but stylish, country-style dining room he serves classical and regional foods with a light, imaginative and innovative accent. This is a warm, friendly establishment that tries hard to please and there is a close attention to detail at every stage. The cooking is of the highest order, though not all of M. Ramelet's creations would be to everyone's taste. For example, we enjoyed the *gâteau de andouille*, the gutsy, local sausage layered with apples and served in a candied, sweet and sour sauce but we dare say this bold, sweet and savoury combination would not be everybody's cup of tea. There are plenty of regional and classic dishes on offer, too, including *cassolette de tripes au cidre* and excellent *confit de canard*, punctuated by an exquisitely light *sorbet* of apple and calvados as the *trou normand*. Desserts are as delicious as they are beautifully presented.

This is a small *auberge* that warrants a detour if you are passing anywhere near. Better still, choose to spend the night in one of three comfortable rooms located in a small annexe that opens on to a lovely and quiet, private garden. The rooms are atmospheric with old flagstone floors and beamed ceilings and are comfortably furnished with full private facilities, telephone, and television.

Closed Tue.; end of Jan. ❖ Credit cards: Visa/CB, Eurocard/Access, American Express, Diners ❖ Menus: 135 F (three courses), 155 F (four courses), 230 F, 280 F ❖ à la carte: about 350–400 F ❖ Rooms: double 335 F, breakfast 37 F ❖ English spoken

Small Hotels and Restaurants

76600 LE HAVRE (SEINE-MARITIME) 🛒
Marché   Tue., Thur., Sat.
Festival   *Fête du Pêcheur*   first weekend in Sept.
Calais 284 km – Rouen 86 km – Paris 204 km

HOTEL

Hôtel Le Marly
121, rue de Paris
76600 Le Havre
tel.: 35 41 72 48
fax: 35 21 50 45

The broad, straight avenues which lead up from the port are all lined with six-story, flat-roofed, concrete blocks of flats built optimistically in the flush of postwar reconstruction. The Marly is located in one such block, wholly characterless, not terribly inviting but conveniently located just a few paces from the ferry terminal. The rooms are rated 3-star but they are frankly no better than adequate, each with shower or bath, w.c., television and telephone. Ask for a room with a concrete balcony overlooking the concrete blocks of Le Havre for a rather singular outlook over the old-fashioned, reconstructed, postwar town.

Open all year ❖ Credit cards: Visa/CB, Eurocard/Access, American Express ❖ Rooms: 340–390 F

RESTAURANT

Le Petit Bedon
37 et 39, rue Louis
Brindeau
tel.: 35 41 36 81
fax: 35 21 09 24

Le Havre is hardly a place where you come to push the boat out: most of us have ended up walking around its confusing maze of streets looking for somewhere decent to eat while trying to kill a few hours before the boat leaves. However, if

you do want a really special meal, you could do far worse than frequent this stylish restaurant located 200 metres from Le Havre's *port de plaisance*. Guy Poyer, proprietor and chef, utilizes the finest Norman produce of both sea and land in a menu that changes with the seasons but which remains imaginative: *boudin de crabe, foie gras normand, saumon fumé maison, langues d'agneau mijotée au vinaigre de cidre*, all

Le Havre

produced and presented in a

light and elegant manner. The best way to sample M. Poyer's creations is with his *menu découvert* which consists of six *dégustations*, punctuated midway, of course, with the *trou normand*.

Closed Sat. midday, Sun.; 1–20 Aug. ❖ Credit cards: Visa/CB, Eurocard/ Access, American Express, Diners ❖ Menus: 155 F, 320 F (*menu découvert*) ❖ à la carte: about 220 F ❖ English spoken

---

RESTAURANT

Restaurant Lescalle

39, place de l'Hôtel de Ville

tel.: 35 43 07 93

Monsieur Hubert has devised a simple but successful formula: a buffet of first courses and a buffet of desserts, punctuated, if you so desire, by basically simple, *brasserie*-style main dishes – *andouillette de Troyes à la graine de moutarde, brochette d'agneau grillé, escalope de volaille normande* – served in the *brasserie*-style interior decorated with frescoes of Bordeaux châteaux, or at pavement tables in fine weather. On Saturday evenings, there are *dîners dansants* which carry on, apparently, until 0200. This comes as something of a surprise to us as every time we have been in Le Havre, virtually the entire town seems to pack up and disappear ridiculously early. So perhaps there are some local night owls.

Closed Sun. evening, Mon., two weeks in Aug. ❖ Credit cards: Visa/CB, Eurocard/Access, American Express ❖ Menus: 70 F, 77 F, 98 F, 115 F, 138 F (at weekends), menu enfant 49 F ❖ English spoken

---

BAR-RESTAURANT

Bar-Restaurant Au Gres d'Alsace

86, rue Victor Hugo

tel.: 35 41 39 83

For those times when you find yourself in Le Havre at the end of your holidays having spent all your money but with the chance to have one last meal, try this simple bar-restaurant that is popular with the locals. In good weather, bask in the sun while enjoying an exceedingly simple, inexpensive, home-cooked menu: a simple *entrée* such as *soupe, terrine maison* or *crudités*, followed by a choice of some four or five *plats du jour* such as *rôti du porc aux pruneaux, lapin aux champignons, tripes à la mode de Caen* or *choucroute*. Wash down this simple repast with a *pichet* of drinkable house wine or with a tumbler of Hoegarden *bière blanche*.

Closed Sun. ❖ Credit cards: Visa/CB, Eurocard/Access ❖ Menus: 60 F, 90 F, 115 F ❖ à la carte: about 100 F

27370 LA HAYE-DU-THEIL (EURE) 🛒
Calais 252 km – Pont-Audemer 32 km – Brionne 15 km

CHAMBRE D'HÔTE

Domaine de la Coudraye

tel.: 32 35 52 07

Luc Damaegdt, a duck and goose farmer, has lived on this beautiful, 200-hectare farm since he was two years old. Today, now that his children have grown up, he has converted two rooms into *chambres* for paying guests. They are both spacious and stylish in a country fashion with wooden floors, high ceilings, big beds and views over the farm. As it is located in the heart of the Eure countryside, this would certainly serve as a nice, peaceful weekend hideaway. Both rooms have their own well-equipped, private bathrooms. Meals are not served here but you could always purchase a jar of the Damaegdt's superlative, home-produced *foie gras* or some *terrine de canard* for a luxury picnic in your room.

Rooms: two persons 220 F including breakfast

Domaine de la Coudraye, La Haye-du-Theil

27500 PONT-AUDEMER (EURE) 🛒

Marché Mon., Fri.

Calais 268 km – Honfleur 25 km – Rouen 50 km

HOTEL-RESTAURANT

**Hôtel-Restaurant
Belle-Isle-sur-Risle**
112, route de Rouen
tel.: 32 56 96 22
fax: 32 42 88 96

The Belle-Isle is located a few kilometres out of the charming and popular, half-timbered tanners' town and situated on its own private island in the middle of the Risle. The tall, five-story mansion, built in 1856 for the owner of a nearby textile factory, sits within its own 5 hectares of grounds in a most idyllic and peaceful, watery situation. This is indeed a very special, luxury, 4-star hôtel-restaurant, run personally and lovingly by the charming and vivacious owner, Madame Marcelle Yazbeck.

In the seven years that she has been here, she has transformed what was a rather dowdy and run-down place into one of the region's top establishments. The twenty luxuriously appointed rooms, some of which have private terraces, have all been completely renovated in individual and personal style reflected in the names of the rooms: Schéhérazade, Louisiane, Océane, Camelia. There is close attention to every detail from the marble bathrooms and luxury, complimentary toiletries to the thick bathrobes, well-stocked mini-bars and comfortable beds. The hotel has a good-sized, outdoor swimming pool, an indoor swimming pool with jacuzzi, and a fitness room; there is, furthermore, a tennis court, tables and benches in the grounds where you can relax and read, a children's play area, even boats in which you can row around the island.

One of the main reasons for staying here, however, is the restaurant under the direction of chef Xavier Ancelot who formerly worked with the Roux brothers in London. This is a serious restaurant with serious prices; yet though the dining room is formal, the atmosphere is relaxed and intimate. Guests who stay on a half-board basis, which is encouraged even if you are only here for a single night, are ususually offered a full choice from the *carte*, though a few dishes require a supplement. Specialities of the house include *panaché de foie gras de canard maison au naturel et aux pommes et sauternes, sandre rôti à la peau aux épices légères* and *pigeonneau en filets laqué au gingembre*. An interesting cheese variation is *sorbet de Roquefort*, the blue cheese mixed with raisins, dates and port wine, then scooped out in balls so that it resembles an ice. Desserts are light and elegant: we especially enjoyed a variation of the upside-down *tarte tatin*, this version being made with ripe but pleasantly sharp mangoes.

All in all, this is a very special hideaway, well worth heading for when you really want to push the boat out for a romantic break or a luxury family weekend away.

Open all year ❖ Credit cards: Visa/ CB, Eurocard/Access, American Express, Diners ❖ Rooms: double 780–1250 F, breakfast 65 F, half– board (dinner, bed & breakfast) 810 F per person ❖ Menus: 190 F (weekdays lunch only), 230 F, 390 F ❖ à la carte: about 300–350 F ❖ English spoken ❖ L S H B

Hôtel-Restaurant Belle-Isle-sur-Risle, Pont-Audemer

CHAMBRE D'HÔTE
AND *TABLE D'HÔTE*

6 km N.E. at Fourmetot

L'Aufragère
La Croisée
tel.: 32 56 91 92
fax: 32 57 75 34

Nicky and Régis Dussartre, an energetic, young couple – she is English, he is French – purchased this 200-year-old, Norman farm in 1992, completely gutted the house, and restored it beautifully, undertaking much of the work themselves. Wherever possible, they have faithfully returned the house to its original state, stripping wood, reinstating half-timbered walls, restoring the old, tiled floors. It has clearly been a labour of love. Today they offer five *chambres* for guests, four with full en suite facilities and one with its own bathroom across the hall. While the rooms on the first floor are decorated in traditional French style, those upstairs in the attic have been decorated in a rather light-hearted, bright style by Nicky using country themes to remind her of her travels around the world before she settled here.

Régis, who is originally from the Limousin, is a farmer by profession and has worked in both France and England. Nicky is a trained, professional chef. Thus the couple offer superior *table d'hôte* meals. A typical menu might start with

gratin de poires au Roquefort, followed by *porc aux pruneaux et calvados*, then a good, local cheeseboard, and finally a homemade dessert. House wine is included, as is the customary *trou normand*.

Nicky runs week-long cookery courses in the winter. Write or fax for details.

Rooms: two persons 210 F including breakfast, 60 F for extra person ❖ Table d'hôte: 100 F ❖ English spoken

Nicky and Régis Dussartre, Fourmetot

76550 POURVILLE-SUR-MER (SEINE-MARITIME)

Calais 180 km – Dieppe 6 km

DÉGUSTATION DES HUÎTRES

L'Huîtrière
rue du 19 août
tel.: 35 84 36 20

The Huîtrière is a *parc à huîtres* where oysters are cultivated in the bay then purified and sold to private customers and restaurateurs. Come here en route to or from Dieppe to sit out on a terrace overlooking the sea in fine weather, to taste exceptional oysters together with chilled bottles of quite passable Muscadet *sur lie*. We find that a dozen *moyennes* at 55 F are more than adequate for a tangy, sea-fresh afternoon snack.

Open daily ❖ à la carte: about 75–100 F

Small Hotels and Restaurants

Marché   Tue., Wed., Fri., Sat.
Calais 218 km – Amiens 114 km – Le Havre 86 km

HOTEL-RESTAURANT

**Hôtel de Dieppe
and Restaurant Les
Quatre Saisons**
place Bernard-Tissot
tel.: 35 71 96 00
fax: 35 89 65 21

Rouen is not the easiest place in which to find a decent hotel with parking near the historic city centre so the Hôtel de Dieppe is a useful find. Located next to the railway station, it is about a ten-minute walk from the cathedral. Now a part of the Best Western chain, the hotel has, in fact, been in Jean-Pierre Gueret's family since 1880. Today, the forty-two soundproofed rooms have all been renovated and each is equipped with private bathroom, w.c., television, telephone, hair dryer and mini-bar. An added reason for staying here is that the Restaurant Les Quatre Saisons, under chef Jacky Folliot Desmeules, is excellent and highly regarded for its traditional Norman cuisine. Indeed, the house speciality is *caneton à la presse*, actually prepared at the table in front of you, and this classic should not be missed.

Open all year ❖ Rooms: 415–585 F, breakfast 40 F or buffet 55 F ❖ Menus: 135 F, 195 F ❖ à la carte: about 220–300 F ❖ English spoken ❖ L S H B

CHAMBRE D'HÔTE

Les Charmilles
2–4, rue Samuel
Bochard
tel.: 35 88 06 38

'We bought this old, historic house in 1976,' explained Marion Delamarre-Tillaux, 'when we were young and very crazy.' She then showed us photos from Rouen newspapers which document how she and her husband Alain restored the medieval, half-timbered edifice just off the Place du Vieux Marché entirely themselves while living there with two small children. The children have now grown up and the Delamarres offer studio *chambres* plus an apartment and a self-contained suite to visitors, for a single night or for longer stays.

The suite has two separate bedrooms, bathroom, a lounge and a kitchenette. It is decorated with old furniture, original paintings by Madame Delamarre's father, bookshelves and comfortable chairs. The apartment, let to students during the academic year but available July to September, is furnished more simply but it is still comfortable and spacious, while the two studio *chambres* are large, each with its own private bathroom and mini-kitchenette. All of the units have

Place du Vieux Marché, Rouen

their own entrance off a central staircase so you can be as private as you like. Madame Delamarre is both warm and dynamic. She is currently working hard to improve her English; she is as delighted to direct you to a good walking tour of the old town as to the best food shops. Considering the central location, the atmosphere of this historic building and the *acceuil* of Madame Delamarre, this certainly must be one of the best accommodation options in town.

Open all year ❖ Rooms: studio *chambres* and apartment (available July–Sept.) two persons 250 F plus 80 F supplement for additional persons; suite two persons 310 F, three persons 390 F, four persons 470 F; all prices include breakfast; there are special tarifs available for weekends, or for stays of more than a few nights ❖ Some English spoken

Small Hotels and Restaurants

CHAMBRE D'HÔTE

Philippe Aunay
45, rue aux Ours
tel.: 35 70 99 68

It is suprising but welcome to find another historic and atmospheric *chambre d'hôte* in Rouen's city centre just a few minutes from its famous and magnificent cathedral. This fascinating, half-timbered dwelling has been in Philippe Aunay's family for over a hundred years. The house itself actually dates from 1602. 'During the period of the French Revolution,' Monsieur Aunay explained, 'it was owned by a royalist. When Louis XVI was guillotined in 1793, he painted the *salle à manger* black.'

Today's decoration is not so glum but it is equally idiosyncratic. Monsieur Aunay is a passionate collector of *objets d'art* and antiques and has filled his house with them. This, then, is a most interesting and fascinating place to stay. The rooms are all individually decorated, mainly with antique furniture, and they are comfortable and clean. There are presently four *chambres*, each with private bath and w.c. The atmospheric, third-floor attic can be rented as an apartment for five or six persons and includes a small kitchenette and lounge.

Open all year ❖ Rooms: two persons 275 F including breakfast; attic apartment 550 F for five persons, 660 F for six persons ❖ English and German spoken

RESTAURANT

La Couronne
31, place du Vieux Marché
tel.: 35 71 40 90
fax: 35 71 05 78

La Couronne claims to be the oldest *auberge* in France having been founded in 1345 and having stayed in virtually continuous operation since then. The English were probably hanging out of its windows and cheering on that fateful day of 30 May 1431 although at least some of them were prescient enough to declare: 'We are lost! We have burnt a Saint.' Don't let our musings put you off your food, though: pause to take in the history and charged atmosphere of this special place while enjoying a superbly prepared *menu du terroir* in elegant and historic surroundings.

This menu changes with the seasons but is refined, regional cuisine and is always based on fresh, local produce: for example, to start either oysters from St-Vaast or the famous Rouennais *charcutier*'s speciality, *pieds de mouton farcis à la rouennaise*, followed by *pêche de petit bateau au cidre normand* or *filet de canard croustillant de pommes aux abats*, then *fromages*, finally a *tarte tatin* served with *crème crue*. All of this

is accompanied by a good, not outrageously priced wine list.

Credit cards: Visa/CB, Eurocard/Access, American Express, Diners ❖ Menus: 150 F, 190 F (including wine), 240 F ❖ à la carte: about 250–350 F ❖ English spoken

La Couronne, Rouen

BISTRO

Les Maraîchers-Bistro d'Adrien

37, place du Vieux Marché

tel.: 35 71 57 73

Sit out under a big, white umbrella at this typical and popular Rouennais *bistro* on the town's main square and enjoy essentially simple foods that rarely disappoint. The cooking is hearty, straightforward and satisfying; the most inexpensive menu offers solid *plats du jour* such as *langue du bœuf sauce piquante*, while on the menu for 135 F you can tuck into a dozen oysters, followed by an *entrecôte* steak, cheese or salad, and a good range of homemade desserts including *gratin de pommes Vallée d'Auge* or delicious *île flottante*. The house wine, served in a *pichet*, costs 55 F a half litre and is drinkable. If it is raining or too cold, come inside and enjoy the busy bustle and magpie decoration of this old, traditional, Norman house.

Open daily ❖ Credit cards: Visa/CB, Eurocard/Access, American Express, Diners ❖ Menus: 87 F, 135 F ❖ à la carte: about 150 F

Small Hotels and Restaurants

76460 ST-VALERY-EN-CAUX (SEINE-MARITIME)
Marché   Fri., Sun. in season
Calais 207 km – Dieppe 34 km – Fécamp 32 km

HOTEL-RESTAURANT

Les Terrasses
22, rue le Perrey sur
Front de Mer
tel.: 35 97 11 22

St-Valery was virtually completely rebuilt after the war so it has little in the way of old character but this is still a popular seaside resort, especially with the French themselves. The chalk cliffs here are as impressive as anywhere along the coast and there is a small marina in the river mouth.

Les Terrasses is one of those old-fashioned, traditional French hotels, located right on the seafront across from a pleasant children's play area on the beach. A basic but comfortable, 2-star *Logis de France*, it offers simply furnished rooms, most with private bath or shower and w.c., some with small terraces opening on to the sea. The restaurant is highly regarded locally for the excellent value of its seafood menus.

Closed Wed.; 20 Dec.–30 Jan. ❖ Credit cards: Visa/CB, Eurocard/Access, Diners ❖ Rooms: 320–350 F, breakfast 35 F ❖ Menus: 130 F, 198 F ❖ à la carte: about 200 F ❖ English spoken

BELGIUM

Belgium, long a curiously neglected tourist destination, is a fascinating and friendly country, rich in history, art and architecture. It has a vital cultural mix and a diversity of peoples which comes from the divide between French-speaking Wallonia and Flemish-speaking Flanders.

Now, through its proximity to the Channel Tunnel and with new international rail services linking London and Brussels, it is high time that we got to know Belgium, not least because there are so many fine places to visit for pleasant and rewarding short breaks.

Flemish-speaking Brugge has long been the most popular tourist destination in the country, and rightly so. This almost wholly intact medieval town is quite unlike anywhere else in Europe. Neglected for centuries after its decline caused by the silting up of its waterways, Brugge is now reaping the benefits, for it has not been spoiled by war damage or thoughtless and unsympathetic development. Rich in Flemish art and architecture, intimate enough to be toured wholly on foot or better still by bicycle, Brugge remains one of the most charming, lovely and enjoyable small towns in northern Europe. There is no shortage of really fine, small hotels which are mostly located in sympathetically reconstructed, period town houses. We are fortunate, indeed, that Brugge is literally on our doorstep.

Gent, on the other hand, is more of a real city than Brugge, less outwardly charming perhaps, yet equally rich in Flemish heritage. It is worth visiting to see the rows of gabled merchants' houses on the Graslei, the grim Castle of the Counts of Gravensteen and, of course, the town's masterpiece by Van Eyck, the Mystic Lamb triptych in the cathedral of Sint-Baaf. Brussels, the nation's capital, is today the seat of the European Parliament and the headquarters of NATO. Officially bilingual, it is an exciting, cosmopolitan place that looks positively to the future. Yet at the same time, Brussels retains something of the feel of a charming, old-world European capital. Come here at weekends, when the businessmen and bureaucrats clear out: the town is definitely more

Damse Vaarte canal, Brugge

manageable then and so are hotel rates.

There are so many fine and inviting places to visit in Belgium. We have space here scarcely to scratch the surface. We enjoy making forays across the now virtually nonexistent Franco-Belgian frontier to places like De Panne on the coast and Poperinge, just across from French Flanders and the Mont des Cats. Chimay is a great, atmospheric brewing town just across the frontier from the lovely Avesnois area of Pas de Calais. Good beers and a warm, country welcome can be had, too, in the Senne valley, south of Brussels, home of gueuze, a unique and wholly individual beer produced by spontaneous, wild fermentation.

As we approach the next millennium, Belgium, long on the periphery of European events, is poised to play a central part in European affairs. This chapter serves as only the briefest of introductions to a country that we should all get to know and enjoy more fully. Now that the Channel Tunnel makes Belgium so easily accessible, we look forward to exploring it much further in the future, and to visiting it again and again.

à Table

French cuisine, say the Belgians, is better in Belgium than in France itself. Certainly this comment is evidence, if any is needed, of supreme Belgian self-confidence as well as an indication of the seriousness and importance of food and drink in everyday life here. Brussels has no fewer than 1,500 restaurants alone; there are stalls and stands on most street corners throughout the country selling waffles and *frites*; on the coast as well as far inland, there is always a bar or café serving that perennial, national favourite *moules-frites*; and throughout, in rural areas and small towns alike, there are scores of simple *auberges* and taverns, *bistros* and roadside cafés, serving the good, inexpensive and hearty foods of the country.

While the foods of the French-speaking parts of Brabant and Hainaut are essentially similar to those found across the border, there are a number of Flemish dishes (known by both Flemish and French names) which have become national favourites. It may be useful to know, therefore, that *carbonnade à la flamande*, the classic beef in beer stew, is known in Flanders variously as *stoverij* or as *vlaamse stoofkarbonaden*; the fishy favourite of

Dish of the day

eels stewed in parsley and other herbs is both *anguilles au vert* and *paling in 't groen*; rabbit stewed in beer can be either *lapin à la bière* or *konijn met bier*; a favourite starter of tiny, sweet, grey shrimps from the North Sea stuffed into tomatoes might appear on menus as either *tomates aux crevettes* or *tomaat garnaal*. *Waterzooï* is, of course, a great national dish, a soupy stew of fish or chicken, cooked with vegetables and finished with cream.

In Flemish-speaking parts of Belgium where the menus are invariably in Flemish you will, in fact, find that almost everybody speaks excellent English. However, this is less true in French-speaking Wallonia. Whether you enjoy fine *haute cuisine* in the French style with a Belgian accent or typically Flemish foods to accompany a range of outstanding beers, one thing is certain: you will always eat well and plentifully, wherever you are in Belgium.

LE MENU DU TERROIR

asperges à la flamande (asperges op vlaamse)
tomates aux crevettes (tomaat garnaal)
Poperingse biersoep
huîtres (oesters)
saumon fumé (gerookte zalm)

anguilles au vert (paling in 't groen)
plie meunière (gebakken schol)
homard au four (kreeftje in de oven)
saumon (zalm)

carbonnade à la flamande (vlaamse stoofkarbonaden, stoverij)
waterzooï
lapin à la gueuze (konijn met gueuze)
jambon d'ardenne

Chimay
St-Bernard
Pas de Bleu

gaufres de liège
glace aux fraises (ijs met aardbeien)
mazarinetaart
crêpes (flensjes)

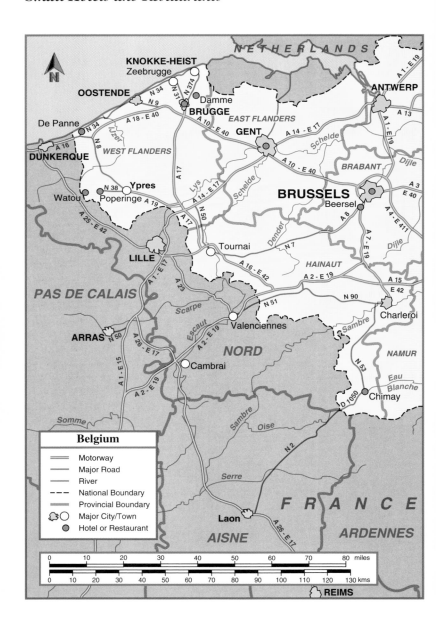

1650 BEERSEL (BRABANT) 🛒

Calais 216 km – Brussels 10 km

BAR-CAFÉ-
RESTAURANT

De Drie Fonteinen
Herman Teirlinckplein 3
tel.: (02) 331 06 52
fax: (02) 331 07 03

In the past, many of the cafés of the Pajottenland – the country south of Brussels where Pieter Bruegel the Elder found inspiration for his Flemish landscapes and lively, peasant scenes – used to produce their own gueuze by purchasing young lambic beers from artisan breweries in the country, then in their own café cellars, aging the beers in wooden casks and eventually blending and bottling them themselves. The Drie Fonteinen is one of few which still undertakes this lengthy, labour intensive task, so a visit here is a must for beer lovers.

Come here to sample by the tall tumbler outstanding gueuze, together with simple drinking snacks such as the classic *plattekaas* (whole-wheat country bread, *fromage frais*, radishes and spring onions) as well as with more considered, complete meals, particularly a range of superlative dishes cooked in beer like *roulade à la gueuze*, *pintadeau à la kriek* or salmon braised with chicory in gueuze. On Thursdays and Fridays, mussels are served in a variety of ways.

If it is not too busy, ask Armand or Guido Debelder, the brothers who own and run the place, if you can see their cellars where the lambic beers are aged in wooden barrels. Incidentally, the kriek served in the café is available either draught or bottled. If you want to taste the real thing, ask for the bottled version, unsweetened, incredibly mouth puckering and tart.

Restaurant closed Tue., Wed. ❖ Credit cards: Visa/CB, Eurocard/Access, American Express, Diners ❖ à la carte: about 500–1,000 BF ❖ English, French and Dutch spoken

Small Hotels and Restaurants

8000 BRUGGE (WEST FLANDERS)

Market   Wed., Sat.

Calais 106 km – Brussels 97 km – Gent 49 km

HOTEL-RESTAURANT

Die Swaene

Steenhouwersdijk
(Groene Rei)

tel.: (050) 34 27 98

fax: (050) 33 66 74

*Koen Hessels,
Die Swaene,
Brugge*

Considering how small Brugge is, the town probably has more characterful, small hotels than virtually anywhere else we know. There are literally scores of really excellent places to stay. People who love this town all have their own favourites. Die Swaene is one of ours. It is quite simply one of the most stylish, friendly and, yes, romantic, little hotels anywhere, warmly run by the entire Hessels family. The hotel is located in three ancient, quayside warehouses which were turned into elegant town houses between the fifteenth and seventeenth centuries. Each of the twenty-three bedrooms is individually and comfortably furnished and equipped to 4-star standard with private bath, w.c., television, telephone and mini-bar; there are rooms with lovely four-poster beds, as well as three large and elegant suites. A small, indoor swimming pool and a tropical garden should be in place by 1994.

The restaurant is equally noteworthy. After drinks and nibbles in the immensely grand, first-floor lounge, which was once the hall of the guild of tailors, diners repair to the intimate and luxuriously romantic, vaulted cellar dining room. Here the cuisine is absolutely first class, precise, classic, and exceedingly fresh, being based on the best produce and products from sea and land: scallops in a truffle sabayon, lobster in a tart *citron* sauce, flavoursome *noisettes d'agneau* in filo pastry, medallions of veal in a redcurrant and truffle sauce. The intelligent wine list is naturally strong on French classics but there are also some interesting, eclectic choices including good Italians such as Castello di Nipozzano as well as some great wines from Spain such as Vega Sicilia, Pesquera, even an off-beat Albariño from Galicia. The only real criticism is that the restaurant is, frankly, very expensive but so are all of Brugge's top establishments. No matter: push out the boat for special occasions, then on alternate nights, 'slum it' in any number of small, welcoming *bistros* and beer taverns in the nearby town centre. The Hessels will most happily advise you on the best ones.

Open all year. Restaurant closed Wed., Thur. midday ❖ Credit cards: Visa/CB, Eurocard/Access, American Express, Diners ❖ Rooms: double 4,850–5,850 BF including buffet breakfast ❖ Menus: 1,700 BF, 2,450 BF ❖ à la carte: about 2,500 BF ❖ Parking in nearby secure car park ❖ English, French, Dutch and German spoken

---

HOTEL

Romantik Pandhotel

Pandreitje 16

tel.: (050) 34 06 66

fax: (050) 34 05 56

The Pandhotel is located in a discreet and elegant, eighteenth-century town house, just a few minutes' walk from the town centre, in a tranquil, residential area. Indeed, the feeling here is that you are staying in your own very stylish, private Brugge residence rather than in a hotel: the twenty-four bedrooms are individually and beautifully decorated, most with period furniture, English fabrics, paintings, antiques and crystal chandeliers and each has excellent facilities, including bath, w.c., television, telephone, mini-bar and hair dryer. In addition to these extremely pretty rooms, there are six spacious, de luxe 'Blossom' rooms as well as two rooms that are suitable for families.

Mrs Chris Dewaele, the owner, is welcoming, hospitable and, as an official guide to the city, extremely knowledgeable about all aspects of Brugge. Ask for details of special, two-night, all-inclusive packages (Romantic and Historic Brugge and Celebration packages).

Open all year ❖ Credit cards: Visa/CB, Eurocard/Access ❖ Rooms: double 4,490 BF, de luxe double 5,990 BF including buffet breakfast ❖ Street parking ❖ English spoken

Small Hotels and Restaurants

HOTEL-RESTAURANT

**Hotel Alfa Dante-
Restaurant
Toermalijn**

Coupure 29a

tel.: (050) 34 01 94

fax: (050) 34 35 39

The Alfa Dante, a modern hotel, is located on the Coupure, a quiet canal. Today there is considerably less water traffic than in bygone days, though huge, flat canal barges still sometimes tie up alongside. This friendly, 4-star hotel has twenty-five spacious rooms which all enjoy lovely views over the canal. Each is equipped with private bath, w.c., television, telephone, mini-bar and hair dryer. All of the rooms are decorated with paintings by the father of Dr Tom Alewaert the owner which give a nice, homely feel to the otherwise modern rooms.

Restaurant Toermalijn is Brugge's best known vegetarian restaurant, located in a light, airy conservatory and serving stylish and delicious, gastronomic wholefoods together with selected organic wines, fruit juices and mineral waters. Young Alain Vanhollebeke is a talented wholefoods chef and he prepares foods with both skill and style. All of the vegetables are organically grown and everything is cooked fresh to order. This is an excellent, mainstream restaurant, popular with people of all ages and backgrounds. 'You know,' says Dr Alewaert, 'many who were hippies in the 1960s today find that we are middle-aged and like comfortable seats as well as quality foods and wines, even if we are vegetarians!' Dr Alewaert is also the owner of the Vlissinghe, one of the oldest and most atmospheric, historic taverns in Brugge: a visit here is a must.

Restaurant closed Sun., Mon.; Feb. and Aug. ❖ Credit cards: Visa/CB, Eurocard/Access, Diners ❖ Rooms: double 5,900 BF including buffet breakfast ❖ à la carte: about 1,200–2,000 BF ❖ Street parking ❖ English, French and Dutch spoken

HOTEL

**Relais Oud Huis
Amsterdam**

Spiegelrei 3

tel.: (050) 34 18 10

fax: (050) 33 88 91

The Oud Huis Amsterdam, located in two mansions dating from the fifteenth and seventeenth centuries which overlook the Spiegelrei canal just up from Jan Van Eyck Plein, is a place of quiet distinction and charm. It is another example of one of Brugge's many fine and individual, family-run hotels which can make a visit to this town such a special experience. The seventeen bedrooms are all spacious, beautifully and tastefully furnished with antiques and original artwork but fully modernized with luxury

bathrooms, some of which have jacuzzis, as well as televisions and telephones. The impression, reported a friend who recently stayed here with his family, is of living in Brugge as it was several centuries ago. The Meeting Bar, located in the seventeenth-century kitchens, is a popular watering hole; there is, furthermore, a fitness room and a quiet garden.

Open all year ❖ Credit cards: Visa/ CB, Eurocard/Access, American Express, Diners ❖ Rooms: 4,500– 6,000 BF including buffet breakfast ❖ English, French, Dutch, Spanish and German spoken

---

HOTEL-*BRASSERIE*

Hotel-Brasserie Erasmus
Wollestraat 35
tel.: (050) 33 57 81
fax: (050) 34 36 30

The Erasmus is a small, reasonably priced hotel in an outstanding, central location just off the main market square. It has a good, informal beer tavern and restaurant. There are only ten rooms, each with private bath, w.c., television, telephone and mini-bar. The decor is, well, kind of funky, with brown, furry bedspreads, but this is a good, comfortable hotel worth knowing, all the same.

The Brasserie is particularly worth singling out. The beer menu runs to three pages and there are over one hundred different brews on offer, all served in their appropriate glasses; the food selection only covers about a quarter of a page, so you know where the priorities are here. Nonetheless, the food that is available is very good, well-prepared and filling, much of it cooked in beer. Come here, then, to gain a good acquaintance with Belgian beers and local foods such as *vlaamse karbonnaden* (*carbonnade à la*

Small Hotels and Restaurants

flamande), *waterzooï van kip* (chicken *waterzooï*), *haantje met Rodenbach* (chicken cooked in sour Rodenbach beer), *konijn met Brigand en graanmosterd* (rabbit cooked in Brigand beer with whole-grain mustard). Such foods provide a good, ample bed for the consumption of copious quantities of Belgian beers.

Brasserie closed Tue. out of season ❖ Credit cards: Visa/CB, Eurocard/Access ❖ Rooms: double 3,700–5,000 BF including buffet breakfast ❖ à la carte: about 600 BF ❖ English spoken

---

HOTEL

Hotel Flanders
Langestraat 38
tel.: (050) 33 88 89
fax: (050) 33 93 45

The Cools family have recently renovated this large, old house on the Langestraat, converting it into a modern and comfortable hotel. There are sixteen rooms which are somewhat on the small side and decorated in cool greens and greys. Our impression is that they are a little characterless in a city whose greatest asset is character. Nonetheless, for the price, each is well equipped with private bath, w.c., television, telephone and even tea and coffee making facilities. Additionally, there are eight small studio flatlets which sleep four to six people and have small kitchenettes. These can be rented for the weekend, a few days mid-week or by the week. A small, indoor swimming pool should keep the kids happy after hours spent pounding the streets of Brugge. One of the hotel's biggest assets is its ample parking in the inner courtyard.

Open all year ❖ Rooms: double 3,750 BF including buffet breakfast, studio flatlet two people for three nights about 9,000 BF ❖ Parking ❖ English spoken ❖ L S H B

HOTEL

Hotel Adornes
St. Annarei 26
tel.: (050) 34 13 36
fax: (050) 34 20 85

This small, budget hotel is just about the nicest and friendliest that we have come across in its price range. Located in a quiet, residential area just a few minutes' walk from Jan Van Eyck Plein, there are twenty comfortable but fairly plain rooms, each of which has private bath and w.c. The largest and nicest rooms are on the ground floor while those in the attic, with atmospheric, beamed ceilings, have a rather cosy feel to them. There is parking and, a real bonus, free use of bicycles. This is by far the best way to get

around Brugge and you can also take excursions along the canal towpath to Damme and beyond. There are a few family rooms available.

Closed Jan.–mid-Feb. ❖ Credit cards: Visa/CB, Eurocard/Access, American Express ❖ Rooms: double 3,300 BF including breakfast ❖ Limited parking available ❖ English, French, German and Spanish spoken

Jan Van Eyck Plein, Brugge

**RESTAURANT
WITH ROOMS**

**'t Bourgoensche
Cruyce**
Wollestraat 41
tel.: (050) 33 79 26
fax: (050) 34 19 68

Brugge has no shortage of first-class restaurants but out of many, 't Bourgoensche Cruyce must rate among the very finest, both for the quality of the innovative French cuisine, and for the intimacy and beauty of the small, classic dining room overlooking the canals just a few steps away from the central market square. Chef Benny Poppe is only thirty-five years old, but he has worked in some of the top restaurants in France including Alain Chapel and brings a fresh and imaginative outlook to this long-standing favourite. The cuisine is strictly seasonal, based on what is freshest each day at market but there is always a strong emphasis on fish and shellfish. *Bouillabaisse* is a house speciality. The six-course *menu dégustation*, which includes wines, is particularly recommended. This is an expensive, luxury restaurant best reserved for special occasions but definitely worth it.

There are also three soberly decorated rooms, all with private facilities and views over the canals.

Closed Tue., Wed. midday; 15 Nov.–15 Dec.; Feb. ❖ Credit cards: Visa/CB, Eurocard/Access, American Express ❖ Menus: 1,450 BF (lunch), 2,160 BF, 3,210 BF (including wines) ❖ à la carte: about 1,500–2,500 BF ❖ Rooms: double 3,200 BF including breakfast ❖ English, French, Dutch and German spoken

RESTAURANT

Restaurant Malpertuus
Eiermarkt 9
tel.: (050) 33 30 38

This atmospheric restaurant, located on the old Egg Market just around from the central market square, is an authentic, *bourgeois* eating house in the old Brugge style. Indeed, at midday, the rather refined, ground-floor dining room seems to be filled mainly with local regulars, old-time residents who like eveything to be just so. More atmospheric and relaxed is the dining room located below in the sixteenth-century, vaulted cellars where you can enjoy such local specialities as fish or chicken *waterzooï*, *paling in 't groen* (eels in green sauce), beef filet with roquefort sauce, rabbit cooked in Trappist beer (be sure to accompany this rich speciality with a goblet of Westmalle tripel). The chef and owner, Mrs De Crom-Puype, has been here for more than twenty years.

Closed Wed. evening, Thur. ❖ Credit cards: Visa/CB, Eurocard/Access, American Express, Diners ❖ Menus: 490–1,050 BF, menu enfant 370 BF ❖ à la carte: about 1,200 BF ❖ English, French, Dutch and German spoken

Restaurant Malpertuus, Brugge

BISTRO

Bistro De Stove
Kleine St-Amandstraat 4
tel.: (050) 33 78 35
fax: (050) 33 79 32

This small *bistro* located just off Brugge's main shopping street, the Steenstraat, is a real find. Whether for an informal lunch or a more considered evening meal, this is a welcoming, small place serving excellent, home-prepared foods. Owner and chef Gino Van Brabant makes everything fresh himself including sauces, soups, desserts, ice cream, even bread and *petit fours*. Come here for good salads, grilled *brochettes*, steaks and fish. Children are very welcome. This is one of the friendliest places we've come across in an altogether friendly city.

Closed Tue. evening in winter, Thur. midday in summer ❖ Credit cards: Visa/CB, Eurocard/Access, American Express, Diners ❖ Menu: 895 BF ❖ à la carte: about 1,200–1,500 BF ❖ English spoken

Bistro De Stove, Brugge

BEER RESTAURANT

Den Dyver
Dyver 5
tel.: (050) 33 60 69

Located centrally on a pretty street leading to the Groeninge and Memling museums, Den Dyver is probably the best beer restaurant in town. Indeed, it is owned and run by a self-confessed beer fanatic, Mr Vandenbusche, who owns the excellent beer tavern De Garre.

De Dyver specializes, purely and simply, in outstanding beer cuisine. Each month there is a set menu with a selection of dishes cooked in a range of beers, all accompanied, of course, by the appropriate beer. On a recent visit, typical and excellent dishes included asparagus salad with beer mousseline sauce served with Steenbruge tripel, *papillote* of sole in a sauce made with Brugse tripel and served with that beer, and for dessert, a light sabayon made with the house beer. There is also a *carte* with a selection of other dishes cooked in beer and some seventy beers to choose from to accompany your meals. The most popular, though, is draught 'n Dievere, brewed in blonde and brown versions especially for the Dyver.

There are outdoor tables where you can enjoy a glass of beer or a cup of coffee with pancakes or ice cream.

Closed Wed. ❖ Credit cards: Visa/CB, Eurocard/Access, American Express, Diners ❖ Beer menu: 1,200 BF (including accompanying beers) ❖ à la carte: about 800–1,500 BF ❖ English spoken

---

BISTRO

Brasserie Belle Epoque
Zuidzandstraat 43
tel.: (050) 33 18 72

The Belle Epoque is located by 't Zand at the end of Brugge's main shopping street. This is a stylish, atmospheric *bistro* decorated in an Art Nouveau style, where you can drop in for a simple snack or an intimate dinner by candlelight. We love the atmosphere, and the cooking is actually very good, too: come here for excellent salads, grilled fish, *brochettes*, a selection of daily specials, and reasonably priced house wines.

Credit cards: Visa/CB, Eurocard/Access, American Express ❖ Menu: 800 BF ❖ à la carte: about 1,000–1,500 BF ❖ English spoken

BREWERY TAVERN

**Hausbrauerei
Straffe Hendrik**
Walplein 26
tel.: (050) 33 26 97
fax: (050) 34 59 35

This outstanding tavern in one of only two working breweries left in Brugge is the place to come for a good 'liquid lunch': bowls of rich, concentrated and flavoursome *biersoep* served with platters of ham and cheese, washed down with a goblet or two of the potent and hoppy Straffe Hendrik beer. The working brewery itself can be toured daily at 1100 and 1500.

Open daily ❖ à la carte: about 500 BF ❖ English spoken

*Straffe Hendrik,
Brugge*

1000 BRUSSELS
Calais 205 km – Brugge 97 km – Lille 105 km

HOTEL-RESTAURANT

**Hôtel Métropole-
Restaurant L'Alban
Chambon**
31, place de Brouckère
tel.: (02) 217 23 00
fax: (02) 218 02 20

The Métropole, constructed in 1895 in the heart of the city and renovated to 5-star, luxury standards, is truly a grand hotel from another era. Vast, decorated in marvellous Art Deco style, and with a genuinely friendly service and old-style attention that seems from another age, the Métropole quite simply provides an experience unlike any other in the city. Indeed, it is rightly regarded affectionately as a Brussels institution. There are over 400 bedrooms, so this is in no way a small, intimate hotel: yet it seems to be run very much along the lines of a family hotel and guests are made to feel very welcome. Each room has full 5-star amenities – spacious private bathroom as large as the bedrooms in many other hotels, separate w.c., thick bathrobes, satellite television, mini-bar, hair dryer, telephone, 24-hour room service.

The restaurant L'Alban Chambon is worth a visit even if you are not staying at the Métropole for it is widely considered to be among the very finest in a city with no shortage of great gastronomic establishments. The dining room is in the old, grand style, with Louis XV decor, French provincial furniture, huge mirrors and high, plastered ceilings. Yet, like the rest of the hotel, service, while impeccably correct, is not overly fussy so the atmosphere remains surprisingly comfortable and relaxed. Chef Dominique Michou prepares classic and neo-classic French cuisine with skilful variety which ranges from original variations of regional, Flemish classics (*ossobucco en waterzooï*) to the Mediterranean (*St-Pierre rôti à plat au parfum d'huile d'olive et jus de ratatouille*). The wine list is extensive and not exhorbitantly priced, while the wine *sommelier* is knowledgable and has a good sense of humour.

Rooms are generally available at favourable rates at weekends. Telephone or fax for details.

Restaurant closed weekends and holidays ❖ Credit cards: Visa/CB, Eurocard/Access, American Express, Diners ❖ Rooms: double 7,500–10,500 BF including breakfast ❖ Menu: 1,350 BF ❖ à la carte: about 1,800–2,500 BF ❖ Parking in front of the hotel or in nearby underground car parks ❖ English, French, Dutch and German spoken

---

HOTEL

Hôtel Manos Residence
100–104, chaussée de Charleroi
tel.: (02) 537 96 82
fax: (02) 539 36 55

This friendly, reasonably priced and relatively small, 4-star hotel has thirty-eight bright and cheerful rooms, each well equipped with bath or shower, television, telephone, mini-bar and hair dryer. The Manos is a discreet and stylish residence located in the quiet, upper part of town off the avenue Louise. Many rooms enjoy pleasant views over the gardens. Mr Emmanuel Poulgouras knows most of his guests personally and there is a warm, family ambience here.

Open all year ❖ Credit cards: Visa/CB, Eurocard/Access, American Express ❖ Rooms: double 3,475–4,275 BF including breakfast ❖ English, French and Italian spoken

HOTEL

Hôtel aux Arcades

36, rue des Bouchers

tel.: (02) 511 28 76

fax: (02) 511 26 52

This small hotel at the top of the rue des Bouchers near the covered Galerie de la Reine is a real find. The location is sensational, just a few minutes' walk from the Grand' Place. There are fifteen cheerfully decorated rooms, some of them reasonably spacious, each with private bath or shower, w.c., television and telephone. There is no restaurant but that hardly matters given its location at the 'stomach' of Brussels on a street lined with literally scores of excellent places to choose from. Come here to enjoy an exciting short break right in the heart of this vital and vibrant European capital.

Open all year ❖ Credit cards: Visa/CB, Eurocard/Access, American Express ❖ Rooms: double 4,100–4,600 BF including breakfast ❖ Nearby underground parking ❖ English spoken

---

RESTAURANT
WITH ROOMS

La Truite d'Argent

23, Quai au Bois à Brûler

tel.: (02) 219 95 46

fax: (02) 217 18 87

The River Senne used to flow through the heart of central Brussels but it has long been diverted underground. The old town *quai* where the boats used to land fish remains an atmospheric old quarter where the *marché aux poissons* takes place. Pleasant fountains along the Quai au Bois à Brûler and the Quai aux Briques create a nice, watery impression. There are scores of superlative fish restaurants, many of which have outdoor tables in fine weather. La Truite d'Argent is certainly among the most popular, a small but elegant, family-run restaurant serving impeccably prepared seafood such as *trilogie de saumon, salade de homard et sa poêlée des pleurotes* and simple, delicious *dorade grillée*.

The Truite has six nicely decorated rooms above the restaurant, each with private bathroom, w.c., television, telephone and hair dryer. This is a delightful area in which to be situated: the Grand' Place is only ten minutes' walk away, the neighbourhood is quiet.

Open all year. Restaurant closed Sun. ❖ Credit cards: Visa/CB, Eurocard/Access, American Express, Diners ❖ Menus: 980 BF, 1,590 BF, 1,950 BF ❖ à la carte: about 1,500 BF ❖ Rooms: 2,100 –2,900 BF ❖ Street parking ❖ English spoken

RESTAURANT

**Auberge des
Chapeliers**
1–3, rue des
Chapeliers
tel.: (02) 513 73 38
fax: (02) 502 21 18

In the narrow streets and lanes leading off from the Grand' Place, there are scores of historic *maisons de corporation* which served as meeting places for workers of various trades. The Auberge des Chapeliers, for example, dates from the seventeenth century and was where the hat makers used to meet after work. Today this busy, friendly, typical eating house, crowded with locals from nearby offices as well as tourists, serves regional and national foods such as *stoemp au lard*, *carbonnades à la flamande*, *waterzooï gantoise*, *steack-frites*, *anguilles au vert* and, of course, *moules-frites* prepared in fifteen different ways. The hectic, *bistro* ambience is authentic, and the welcome here from owners Mr and Mrs de Smaele is warm and genuine.

Open daily ❖ Credit cards: Visa/CB, Eurocard/Access, American Express, Diners ❖ Menus: 480–995 BF ❖ à la carte: about 1,000 BF ❖ English, French and Dutch spoken

Grand' Place, Brussels

RESTAURANT

Chez Léon

18–22, rue des
Bouchers

tel.: (02) 511 14 15

Chez Léon started life over a hundred years ago as the only bar on the rue des Bouchers serving the now classic national stand-by *moules-frites*. Today, there are probably more than eighty competitors in the vicinity, for this street and its adjoining alleys have become known as the 'stomach' of Brussels, the place where locals come to eat. Chez Léon, always full night or day, continues to satisfy a discerning clientèle by sticking to the basics: *moules* served in about a dozen different ways, good Belgian dishes, grilled, fresh fish and tasty, inexpensive *plats du jour*, accompanied by reasonable house wine and beers.

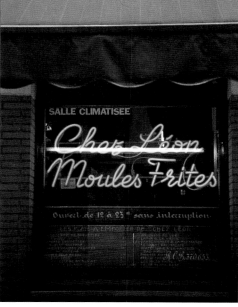

Open daily ❖ Credit cards: Visa/CB, Eurocard/Access, American Express, Diners ❖ à la carte: about 750–1,000 BF ❖ English spoken

Chez Léon, Brussels

BISTRO

Au Stekerlapatte

4, rue des Prêtres

tel.: (02) 512 86 81

fax: (02) 514 27 72

This friendly *bistro* has a warm, bohemian atmosphere that is typical of old Brussels. Classic *bistro* cuisine is prepared by chef Ahsan Ahmad: superb *croquettes aux crevettes grises*, unctuous *pieds de cochon* and favourites like *l'onglet aux échalotes*, *lapin grande-mère*, *l'île flottante*. There is a good wine list with most bottles at less than 1,000 BF.

Open Tue.–Sun. evenings only ❖ Credit card: Visa/CB ❖ Menus: 1200 BF (wine and coffee included), menu enfant 500 BF ❖ à la carte: about 1,200 BF ❖ English, French, Dutch and German spoken

RESTAURANT

Bij den Boer
60, Quai aux Briques
tel.: (02) 512 61 22

The many fish restaurants along the Quai aux Briques and the Quai au Bois à Brûler are, on the whole, fine for an evening out, less useful for a simple midday meal. This old, typical tavern is something of a find, therefore, a really authentic local that is friendly, untouristy, and serves excellent, home-cooked foods. It is always full at midday with workers and nearby residents enjoying huge bowls of *moules, tomates crevettes*, excellent *sole meunière, anguilles au vert* or the daily seafood *plat du jour*, washed down with tall glasses of Stella Artois or golden goblets of Duvel. When we were last here the locals were all tucking into plates of *orphie*, a type of eel only available in May. Madame Breckx-Valck, who originally comes from the Pajottenland, has been serving regulars for twenty-six years; after she finishes cooking, she comes out to greet her customers most of whom are old friends.

Bij den Boer,
Brussels

Closed Sun., Mon. evening, Tue. evening, Sat. evening, holidays ❖ No credit cards ❖ à la carte: about 750 BF

TAVERN-RESTAURANT-
MICRO-BREWERY

Café Le Miroir

24–26, place Reine
Astrid
tel.: (02) 424 04 78
fax: (02) 424 22 01

Jean-Jacques and Jean-Paul Cox have revived the tradition of café brewing that was once common in the capital by creating Brussel's first combined café and micro-brewery. Here in Jette, a suburb in the northwest part of town, the brothers have now begun to brew distinctive, unpasteurized and characterful beers in a modern and well-equipped micro-brewery actually within the café itself for customers to consume *sur place* while enjoying both typical *brasserie* and regional foods as well as *cuisine à la bière*. Two beers are currently produced: Spéciale Miroir Blanche and Spéciale Miroir Dark. There is also a good range of other artisan Belgian beers on offer, most notably the outstanding range of gueuze, kriek and faro from Cantillon, the last gueuze brewery in Brussels, and the genuine (and virtually unobtainable) Sint-Sixtus Trappist beers brewed at the abbey at Westvleteren. The food is better than normal 'pub grub' and includes typical dishes such as *carbonnades à la flamande au faro*, rabbit stewed in the dark Miroir beer, and *médaillons de lotte* cooked in gueuze. The selection of wines on offer is not bad, either. Worth a visit.

Open daily ❖ Menus: 450 BF (lunch weekdays only), menu enfant 290 BF ❖ à la carte: about 500 BF ❖ English spoken

6480 CHIMAY (HAINAUT) 🛒
Calais 218 km – Brussels 95 km – Avesnes-sur-Helpe 30 km

TAVERN-RESTAURANT

*8 km S. at
Scourmont*

**Auberge de
Poteaupré**

5, rue Poteaupré
tel.: (060) 21 14 33

This country inn near the Abbey of Scourmont, home of the famous, Trappist Chimay beer is the place where beer pilgrims come to sample at the source, or as close to the source as you can get, the abbey brewery itself being off-limits. Come here to join the crowds (there is usually a coachload or two here) and to enjoy goblets filled with foaming red-top, white-top or – strongest and most distinctive – blue-top Chimay ales, accompanied by quite substantial meals such as *lapin à la bière des Trappistes*, *rôti de porc à la chimacienne*, *escavèche du pays*, and platters of Chimay cheeses.

Since the abbey beers tend towards the strong and the very strong, we certainly wouldn't suggest that you even consider driving if you've had even one or two. Better to

*Auberge de
Poteaupré, Chimay*

hole up here for the night in one of the eleven bedrooms which are extremely simple, plain, almost monastic in feel but which have their own private facilities. This would make a very peaceful retreat, provided things don't get too out of hand in the bar down below.

Open daily July–Aug., closed Mon. ❖ Credit cards: Visa/CB, Eurocard/Access ❖ Menu: 850 BF ❖ à la carte: about 750–1,000 BF ❖ Rooms: double 700–1,300 BF including breakfast ❖ Parking ❖ English spoken

8340 DAMME (WEST FLANDERS)
Calais 113 km – Brugge 7 km

RESTAURANT

*2 km N. at
Oostkerke*

Restaurant Siphon
Damse Vaart Oost 1
tel.: (050) 62 02 02

Damme

The Siphon is located just beyond Damme where the Damse Vaarte meets two other canals in the middle of the flat, weirdly beautiful *polder* landscape. This immense eating house is a remarkable operation, heaving with regulars at weekends who come here not only from Brugge but from throughout the surrounding countryside. This is still a wholly family-run establishment specializing, above all, in Flemish eel dishes (particularly the famous *paling in 't groen*), followed by T-bone steaks and other meats grilled over a wood-fire in the dining room. Frank Callewaert, known as 'Frankie' to all the regulars, says, 'My mother is the chef. It is only with difficulty that she lets me replace her occasionally.' Come out here not only for outstanding if essentially basic foods but also to see how the Belgians live and enjoy themselves in the country. We have enjoyed cycling here from Brugge, eating the local specialities, then continuing

along the canal towpath into nearby Holland. Why not rent a bike and do the same?

Closed Thur.; 1–16 Feb.; 1–16 Oct. Essential to book at weekends ❖ No credit cards (Eurocheques accepted) ❖ à la carte: about 1,000–1,500 BF ❖ English, French, German and Dutch spoken

---

8660 DE PANNE (WEST FLANDERS)
Calais 63 km – Brugge 55 km – Oostende 30 km

HOTEL-RESTAURANT

Hostellerie Le Fox

Walckiersstraat 2
tel.: (058) 41 28 55
fax: (058) 41 58 79

Belgium's seventy-odd kilometres of North Sea coastline claim to be some of the best in northern Europe. Certainly the beaches are vast, clean and sandy. However, if you come here in July or August, it is difficult to get anywhere near them, so popular is the coast not only with the Belgians but also with the Dutch, Scandinavians and Germans.

De Panne is the closest resort to France and England. The wide beach and spectacular and still unspoiled sand dunes are certainly excellent, and the busy, little town is hectic and fun. It is worth coming here, too, to stay at Le Fox, which is probably De Panne's best 4-star hotel, certainly the home of one of its best restaurants. Located just off the seafront, the hotel has eleven double rooms, all with private facilities, cable television, telephone and mini-bar. Some have a side view of the sea, while the quietest are in the back. The highly regarded restaurant serves sensational fish and shellfish and seasonal specialities such as asparagus.

Closed Oct.; 16–30 Jan. ❖ Credit cards: Visa/CB, Eurocard/Access, American Express, Diners ❖ Rooms: 2,500–2,700 BF, breakfast 250 BF ❖ Menus: 1,750 BF (four course), 2,350 BF (five course), 3,200 BF (five course including wines) ❖ à la carte: about 2,000 BF ❖ English, French, Dutch and German spoken

9000 GENT (EAST FLANDERS) 🛒

Market   Fri., Sat.
Festival   Gent Festival   About third weekend in July
Calais 172 km – Brussels 56 km – Brugge 49 km

HOTEL-RESTAURANT

Cour St-Georges
St Jorishof
Botermarkt 2
tel.: (09) 224 24 24
fax: (09) 224 26 40

The Cour St-Georges, founded in 1228, is considered to be the oldest hotel in Europe still in continuous operation; indeed, much of the history of this once centrally important, Flemish town is preserved within its walls. The great, Gothic hall, today the dining room of the restaurant, was where in 1477 Mary of Burgundy signed a famous charter which granted independence to all Flemish cities. The Emperor Charles V regularly stayed here and Napoleon spent two nights here in 1805.

Sadly, since 1990, the bedrooms in Cour St-Georges have been closed so guests now stay in the St-Jorishof annexe just across the road where there are twenty-eight bedrooms and two spacious mini-apartments which were recently redecorated and have full private facilities, television, telephone and mini-bar. St-Jorishof is an atmospheric, eighteenth-century mansion that was once the headquarters of the St-Jorishof guild of archers whose members constituted a private army for the protection of the Counts of Flanders.

The restaurant is worth visiting even if you are not staying here. The Gothic hall, with its wooden panelling, monumental fireplace, beamed ceiling, heavy, iron chandeliers, coats of arms and oak furniture is, indeed, an impressive and grand eating hall, noted for centuries for the excellence of its kitchen. Come here, then, to enjoy an excellent, first-class restaurant serving both classic French cuisine as well as hearty but well-presented, Flemish specialities – *paling in 't groen*, *gentse waterzooï*, rabbit cooked in beer, asparagus Flemish style – accompanied by a good, reasonably priced selection of mainly French wines. An excellent Sunday brunch is served in season.

Open all year. Restaurant closed Sun. evening ❖ Credit cards: Visa/CB, Eurocard/Access, American Express, Diners ❖ Rooms: double 3,300–3,900 BF including breakfast. Apartment 5,500 BF ❖ Menus: 920 BF, 1,100 BF, menu enfant 650 BF ❖ à la carte: about 1,500 BF ❖ Parking ❖ English, French, German and Dutch spoken ❖ L S H B

Small Hotels and Restaurants

HOTEL

Hotel Gravensteen
Jan Breydelstraat 35
tel.: (09) 225 11 50
fax: (09) 225 18 50

Near the grim, 800-year-old Castle of Gravensteen and just a few steps away from the atmospheric and attractive Patershol quarter, this grand, 4-star hotel is located in a patrician's mansion dating from the middle of the nineteenth century. The hotel has been entirely renovated in Second Empire style. The seventeen bedrooms are comfortable if not overly luxurious, each well equipped with full private facilities, television, telephone and mini-bar. There is a small bar, 'The Donjon', a garden and a penthouse belvedere which affords superb views over the castle and the famous towers of Gent. The Gravensteen offers attractive weekend packages throughout the year: write or fax for details.

Open all year ❖ Credit cards: Visa/CB, Eurocard/Access, American Express, Diners ❖ Rooms: double 3,900–4,500 BF including buffet breakfast ❖ Parking ❖ English, French, Dutch, German and Spanish spoken

Hotel Gravensteen, Gent

HOTEL

Hotel Erasmus
Poel 25
tel.: (09) 224 21 95
fax: (09) 333 42 41

Located in the heart of old Gent, this recently converted, sixteenth-century patrician house is the best small hotel that we have found. Mr and Mrs Coone-Verbrugghen have completely renovated this old, traditional residence doing much of the work themselves and they have created a stylish and individual hotel with eleven bedrooms, each with private bath, w.c., television and telephone. The rooms are

Hotel Erasmus, Gent

all individually and personally decorated, some with antique furniture, others with personal items, and they are all extremely homely and comfortable. The old, beamed dining room serves as a bright and cheery breakfast room where substantial buffet breakfasts are served, and there is a pleasant garden terrace where drinks can be taken in fine weather.

Credit cards: Visa/CB, Eurocard/Access, American Express ❖ Rooms: double 2,975–3,175 BF including breakfast ❖ English spoken

---

RESTAURANT

Restaurant Graaf Van Egmond

Sint-Michielshelling 21

tel.: (09) 225 07 27

fax: (09) 225 18 32

The Graaf Van Egmond overlooks Gent's Graslei which is lined with splendid, gabled guild houses dating from the twelfth, thirteenth, fourteenth and fifteenth centuries. It is actually located in one of the town's most beautiful, medieval, stone mansions, built in 1200 with façade and interior remodelled in 1662 in the Flemish Renaissance style. The restaurant has long been something of a Gent institution, though locals say that today the food is only adequate at best. It is worth coming here, all the same, to enjoy the splendid views over the water to the towers of the town. The ground-floor restaurant serves classic French cuisine, while the first-floor restaurant, which enjoys the best views, serves traditional foods of Flanders and Burgundy. There is a range of moderately priced menus which includes all the classics – *paling in 't groen, gentse stoverij, waterzooï.*

Credit cards: Visa/CB, Eurocard/Access, American Express, Diners ❖ Menus: from 370–1,025 BF, children eat at half price ❖ à la carte: about 1,000–1,500 BF ❖ English, French, Dutch, German, Spanish and Italian spoken

---

RESTAURANT

Raadskelder
Botermarkt 18
tel.: (09) 225 43 34
fax: (09) 224 05 89

Raadskelder, Gent

The Raadskelder is located in the cellar of the Lakenhalle or linen hall built in 1425, beside the town's famous belfry which served in medieval times as the gathering place for the town's textile merchants. Today, this is a large, atmospheric, informal restaurant with a low, cross-vaulted dining room lined with massive pillars which support the great hall above. There are coats of arms on the walls, a low, lacquered ceiling, heavy, iron candlestands and dark, carved-wood furniture. To be honest, it's just a little dark and oppressive, a rather vast, echoing place when only half full. But it is a fascinating venue all the same: a place not to come to for inspired *haute cuisine*, but rather to enjoy well-

prepared, Flemish specialities – *paling in 't groen, stoverij* and *gentse waterzooï* – served in unique and historic surroundings.

Open daily ❖ Credit cards: Visa/CB, Eurocard/Access, American Express, Diners ❖ Menus: 540–900 BF ❖ à la carte: about 750 BF ❖ English, French, Dutch and German spoken

---

RESTAURANT

Chez Léon
Korenmarkt 4
tel.: (09) 225 48 88

Chez Léon started over a hundred years ago as a simple bar in Brussels serving the now classic *moules-frites*: today there are branches in a number of cities including Paris. This one, centrally and conveniently located on the Korenmarkt, may not have quite the busy ambiance of its counterpart in Brussels but it is a useful place to come to all the same for *moules-frites*, good Belgian dishes as well as tasty and inexpensive *plats du jour*.

Open daily ❖ Credit cards: Visa/CB, Eurocard/Access, American Express, Diners ❖ à la carte: about 500 BF ❖ English spoken

---

RESTAURANT

Amadeus
Plotersgracht 8
tel.: (09) 225 13 85
333 27 74

The Patershol quarter, located near the castle, is a medieval, working-class neighbourhood once populated by artisans and tradesmen: today the terrace houses which date from the sixteenth, seventeenth and eighteenth centuries are being restored. This area is in the process of being

transformed into an atmospheric, charming quarter with lots of good, small restaurants. Amadeus is a typical and raucous eating house that is always popular and crowded. Come here for one thing only: racks of spareribs – as much as you can eat – grilled over an open fire and served on a wooden platter with baked potatoes and salad. The 1.5-litre bottle of house red on each table is quite quaffable and you are only charged for

*Castle of
Gravensteen, Gent*

what you consume. There are usually student musicians who add to the generally boisterous and bohemian atmosphere.

No credit cards ❖ Menu: 650 BF ❖ à la carte: about 500 BF ❖ English spoken

---

8970 POPERINGE (WEST FLANDERS) 🛒

Market   Fri.
Festival   International Hop Festival   Every three years (next in 1996)
Calais 80 km – Ypres 12 km – Brugge 64 km – Lille 45 km

HOTEL-RESTAURANT

Hotel-Restaurant Amfora
Grote Markt 36
tel.: (057) 33 88 66
fax: (057) 33 88 77

Poperinge, located just a few kilometres inside the Franco-Belgian border looking across to the Mont des Cats of French Flanders, is one of the principle hop-growing areas in Belgium, so a visit here is a must for serious lovers of beer. The National Hop Museum is certainly worth visiting and there is a sign-posted 'Hoppeland' route which leads through the hop gardens of the surrounding countryside with many excellent stops at local inns (ask at the Information Office for details). This small corner of Belgium suffered greatly during the First World War. Some of the fiercest, bloodiest trench warfare took place here and around nearby Ypres and Passchendaele. The Lyssenthoek Military Cemetery, beautifully maintained by the Commonwealth War Graves Commission amidst the hop gardens, is a poignant reminder: nearly 11,000 young men are buried here, where 'In Flanders fields the poppies blow/ Between the crosses, row on row ...'

The Amfora is located on Poperinge's market square in a doctor's house dating from turn of the century. It is probably the best small hotel in town, owned and run by Trui Riquière-Vroman and her husband Martial who is a renowned, local chef. There are only seven newly converted rooms here, but each is spacious and well appointed and enjoys private bath and w.c., television, telephone, mini-bar and hair dryer.

The Amfora is best known for its stylish and excellent restaurant where Martial prepares mainly French cuisine with a Flemish accent, utilizing local produce and products. In spring, for example, there is an asparagus menu. Local foods include *Poperingse biersoep* (made with the local, bitter

Hommelbier), while more refined dishes also feature, such as homemade *ganzelever (foie gras)* and *kreeftje in de oven* (baked lobster).

Additionally, there is an informal tavern which is extremely popular, serving a good range of Belgium beers accompanied by simple foods and drinking snacks such as *Poperingse hennepot* (chicken, rabbit and veal set in a cold, sharp jelly) and salads as well as some good, daily specials.

Restaurant closed Sun. evening, Wed. ❖ Credit cards: Visa/CB, Eurocard/ Access, American Express, Diners ❖ Rooms: double 2,200–3,000 BF including buffet breakfast ❖ Restaurant menus: *Toeristen* menu (includes regional dishes and beers) 1,300 BF; *Degustatie* menu 2,750 BF (seven courses including wines) ❖ Taverne menu: about 1,000 BF (including a glass of wine) ❖ à la carte: about 1,500 BF ❖ English, French, Dutch and German spoken

---

FARMHOUSE
BED & BREAKFAST
WITH *TABLE D'HÔTE*

Aan de Schreve
Bethunestraat 15
tel.: (057) 33 41 79

Aan de Schreve is a large, Flemish farm located outside Poperinge about half a kilometre from the French frontier near the Lyssenthoek Military Cemetery, looking across to the Mont des Cats and French Flanders. This is an extremely peaceful place to stop, a working farm where Mr and Mrs Vansuyt offer seven very basic but clean and comfortable rooms (shared bath and w.c. facilities only). Evening meals are available on request and consist of home-cooked foods

Aan de Schreve,
Poperinge

utilizing the produce of the farm. There is always an ample farmhouse breakfast served at the large, communal trestle table where all the guests sit together. In warm weather, there are pleasant tables in the courtyard where you can have a drink and this area can also be used for barbeques. There is a large playground for children.

Open all year ❖ Rooms: two persons 1,600 BF including breakfast. Children under ten 600 BF, children under three 400 BF ❖ Table d'hôte: about 400 BF

TAVERN
AND TEA HOUSE

Taverne Cyrus
Leperrstraat 108
tel.: (057) 33 81 26

This typical tavern and tea shop, named after Poperinge's famous giant (a huge model brought out for processions and carnivals), is a friendly and convenient stop. This historic, beamed building is owned and run by Luk Dequidt and his charming wife Jeanien. This is a good place to come for a glass of local Hommelbier and an open sandwich, a plate of spaghetti or a cup of coffee and a slice of warm, homemade apple pie or the famous Poperinge mazarine cake, a sponge soaked in a rich butter and cinamon mix. Luk is the Poperinge tourist officer, so if he is not in the Cyrus you can probably find him in the Information Office: he knows everyone and everything about the place and is extremely helpful. Luk can advise you where to go, where to stay and what to see, and will also explain some of the local beers, preferably over a glass or two.

Closed Wed. ❖ à la carte: about 500 BF ❖ English, Dutch, German and French spoken

---

RESTAURANT

8 km W. at Watou

't Hommelhof
Watouplein 17
tel.: (057) 38 80 24
fax: (057) 38 85 90

Watou, a small town virtually on the border and not far from Poperinge, stands in the middle of the hop country and is a noted brewing centre, home of two important and highly regarded breweries, St Bernardus and Kapitell. So important is beer in the daily scheme of local life that there is even a brewer's statue on the little market square.

This rustic restaurant dating from 1600 is located in the square and is noted, above all, for its high quality, gastronomic cuisine and a range of superlative, traditional and imaginative dishes all prepared with different beers. The house speciality is lobster cooked in beer. Naturally, all of the dishes can be accompanied by their respective beers. This is certainly a place for real beer lovers to hunt out.

Closed Mon. evening, Wed., Thur. evening; 22 Dec.–10 Jan. Open daily July and Aug. ❖ Credit cards: Visa/CB, Eurocard/Access, American Express ❖ à la carte: about 1,700 BF, menu enfant 500 BF ❖ English, Flemish, French, German and Dutch spoken

INDEX OF PLACES AND ESTABLISHMENTS

Names of hotels, restaurants, etc. appear in *italics*. Names of hotels which can be booked through Le Shuttle Holidays' Breaks 1994 programme appear in **bold**.

Aan de Schreve, Poperinge, 183
Abbeville, 84
Adornes, Brugge, 162
Aguado, Dieppe, 131
Alfa Dante-Toermalijn, Brugge, 160
Amadeus, Gent, 181
Ambonnay, 108
Amfora, Poperinge, 182
Amiens, 85–87
Andelys, Les, 130
Arcades, Brussels, 169
Ardres, 21–22
Armes de Champagne, L'Epine, 115
Arras, 23–24
Arts, Le Touquet, 73
Atlantic, Wimereux, 76
Audinghen, 24–26
Audresselles, 27
Aufragère, Fourmetot, Pont-Audemer, 146
Aunay, Rouen, 150
Avesnes-sur-Helpe, 27

Baie-Mado, Le Crotoy, 93
Bannière de France, Laon, 96
Baron, Gussignies, 45
Bas Loquin, 52
Beau Lieu, Forges-les-Eaux, 141
Beau Sarrazin, Fontaine-sur-Aÿ, 115
Beersel, 157
Belle Epoque, Brugge, 166
Belle-Isle-sur-Risle, Pont-Audemer, 145
Bellevue, Lille, 52
Berceaux, Epernay, 113

Bergues, 28
Bij den Boer, Brussels, 172
Bistro 191, Senlis, 102
Bistro d'Adrien, Rouen, 151
Boeschepe, 29
Bœufs, Germaine, 116
Bony, 88
Bouchon, Compiègne, 93
Boulogne-sur-Mer, 30–34
Bourgoensche Cruyce, Brugge, 163
Boyer Les Crayères, Reims, 118
Bretagne, St-Omer, 65
Brionne, 130
Briquet, Lewarde, 51
Briqueterie, Vinay, 123
Brueghel, Lille, 53
Brugge, 158–167
Buffet de France, Abbeville, 84

Calais, 34–37
Cambrai, 37–39
Campanile, Chantilly, 89
Campanile, Reims, 120
Cap Gris Nez, Audinghen, 25–26
Cap, Escalles, 41
Capelette, Etrœungt, 27
Capitainerie, Chantilly, 90
Cappy, 88
Caveau, Cumières, 111
Cèdre, Noyon, 98
Chaîne d'Or, Les Andelys, 130
Champillon Bellevue, 109
Channel, Calais, 36
Chantilly, 89–91
Chapeliers, Brussels, 170

Charmilles, Rouen, 148
Château de Cocove, Recques-sur-Hem, 63
Château de la Motte Fénelon, Cambrai, 37
Château des Tourelles, Le Wast, 74
Château Tilques, Tilques, St-Omer, 68
Châtillon-sur-Marne, 110
Cheval Blanc, Sept-Saulx, 123
Chez Léon, Brussels, 171
Chez Léon, Gent, 181
Chez Mimi, Audresselles, 27
Chimay, 173
Clairmarais, 67–68
Clément, Ardres, 21
Clos du Montvinage, Etreaupont-en-Thiérache, 94
Cœur de Lion, Brionne, 130
Compiègne, 91–93
Coquille, Lille, 55
Cour St-Georges, Gent, 177
Couronne, Rouen, 150
Créquy, 44
Crotoy, Le, 93
Crystal, Reims, 119
Cumières, 111
Cygne, St-Omer, 66
Cyrus, Poperinge, 184

Damme, 175
Darnétal, Montreuil-sur-Mer, 62
De Panne, 176
Delabie, Boulogne-sur-Mer, 34

Desvres, 39
Dieppe, 131–136
Dieppe, Rouen, 148
Domaine de la Coudraye,
    La Haye-du-Theil, 144
Domaine des Oiseaux,
    Rosnay, 121
Donjon, Etretat, 138
Drie Fonteinen, Beersel, 157
Duclair, 136
Dunkerque, 40
Dyver, Brugge, 165

Epernay, 113–114
Epine, L', 115
Epsom, Dieppe, 132
Erasmus, Brugge, 161
Erasmus, Gent, 178
Escale de Cappy, Cappy, 88
Escalles, 41–42
Escargot, Cambrai, 39
Etaples, 43
Etreaupont-en-Thiérache,
    94–95
Etretat, 138–139
Etrœungt, 27

Faisanderie, Arras, 24
Fécamp, 139
Ferme du Vert,
    Wierre-Effroy, 75
Flanders, Brugge, 162
Flandres, Hesdin, 48
Fontaine-sur-Aÿ, 115
Forges-les-Eaux, 141
Fourmetot, 146
Fox, De Panne, 176
France,
    Montreuil-sur-Mer, 60
France-Chat qui Tourne,
    Compiègne, 91
Fruges, 44

Galamez, Clairmarais,
    St-Omer, 67
Gent, 177–182

George V, Calais, 34
Germaine, 116
Goûter Champêtre,
    Chantilly, 91
Graaf Van Egmond,
    Gent, 179
Grand Cerf,
    Montchenot, 117
Grand Duquesne, Dieppe,
    133
Grand' Maison, Escalles, 42
Gravensteen, Gent, 178
Grenouillère, Madeleine-
    sous-Montreuil, 62
Gres d'Alsace, Le Havre, 143
Grillade, Epernay, 114
Gussignies, 45

Hamiot,
    Boulogne-sur-Mer, 33
Hardelot, 46–47
Hauts de Montreuil,
    Montreuil-sur-Mer, 59
Havre, Le, 142–143
Haye-du-Theil, La, 144
Hesdin, 48
Hommelhof, Watou,
    Poperinge, 184
Huîtrière,
    Boulogne-sur-Mer, 32
Huîtrière, Etretat, 139
Huîtrière, Lille, 54
Huîtrière,
    Pourville-sur-Mer, 147

Ibis Centre, Lille, 54
Igny Comblizy, 117
Inxent, 49
Inxent, Inxent, 49

Jolimetz, 50
Jules, Desvres, 39

Laon, 96
Leclerq, Lille, 55
Lescalle, Le Havre, 143

Lewarde, 51
Licques, 51–52
Lille, 52–56
Loison-sur-Créquoise, 56
Lorraine,
    Boulogne-sur-Mer, 30
Louches, 22
Lumbres, 57
Lutterbach, Lille, 55

Madeleine-sous-Montreuil,
    62
Maison de la Houve,
    Audinghen, 24
Maison du Perlé, Loison-sur-
    Créquoise, 56
Malpertuus, Brugge, 164
Manoir de la Renardière,
    Erondelle, Abbeville, 84
Manoir de Montflambert,
    Mutigny, 118
Manoir du Brugnobois,
    Surques, 51
Manoir du Rouge Camp,
    Louches, 22
Manos Residence,
    Brussels, 168
Marissons, Amiens, 86
Marly, Le Havre, 142
Marmite Dieppoise,
    Dieppe, 134
Maroilles, 58
Matelote,
    Boulogne-sur-Mer, 31
Mauves, Cap Gris Nez,
    Audinghen, 25
Mélie, Dieppe, 134
Mercure, Péronne, 98
Métropole,
    Boulogne-sur-Mer, 30
Métropole, Brussels, 167
Meunerie, Téteghem, 40
Miroir, Brussels, 173
Moniteur, Calais, 36
Montchenot, 117
Montreuil-sur-Mer, 59–63

Small Hotels and Restaurants

Mormal, Jolimetz, 50
Moulin de Mombreux,
    Lumbres, 57
Mutigny, 118

Nausicaa,
    Boulogne-sur-Mer, 31
Nénuphars, Clairmarais, 68
Noyon, 97–98

Océan, Hardelot, 47
Oostkerke, 175
Oud Huis Amsterdam,
    Brugge, 160

Parc, Hardelot, 46
Pêcheurs d'Etaples,
    Boulogne-sur-Mer, 33
Pêcheurs d'Etaples, Etaples, 43
Péronne, 98
Petit Bedon, Le Havre, 142
Peupliers, Bas Loquin,
    Licques, 52
Plage, Wissant, 77
Polo, Le Touquet, 73
Pont-Audemer, 145–147
Poperinge, 182
Port et des Bains, St-Valery-
    sur-Somme, 100
Port, Dieppe, 135
Porte Oubliée,
    Châtillon-sur-Marne,
    110
Poste, Duclair, 136
Poteaupré, Scourmont,
    Chimay, 173
Pourville-sur-Mer, 147

Raadskelder, Gent, 180
Rabaude, Staple, 71

Recques-sur-Hem, 63
Red Fox, Le Touquet, 72
Reims, 118–121
Relais des 4 Saisons, St-
    Valery-sur-Somme, 100
Relais Guillaume de Normandy,
    St-Valery-sur-Somme,
    99
Relais, Ardres, 21
Romantik Pandhotel,
    Brugge, 159
Rosnay, 121
Rouen, 148–152
Royal Champagne,
    Champillon Bellevue,
    109
Ru Jacquier, Igny
    Comblizy, 117

St-Eloi, Noyon, 97
St-Louis, St-Omer, 66
St-Omer, 65–70
St-Valery-en-Caux, 152
St-Valery-sur-Somme,
    99–101
St-Vincent, Ambonnay, 108
Sapinière, Wisques,
    St-Omer 70
Sauvage, St-Valery-sur-
    Somme, 101
Scourmont, 173
Senlis, 102
Sept-Saulx, 123
Serge Pérard, Le Touquet, 73
Siphon, Oostkerke,
    Damme, 175
Sire de Créquy, Créquy, 44
Sirène, Cap Gris Nez,
    Audinghen, 26
Sole Meunière, Calais, 36

Staple, 71
Stekerlapatte, Brussels, 171
Stove, Brugge, 165
Straffe Hendrik, Brugge, 167
Surques, 51
Swaene, Brugge, 158

Table en Périgord, Reims, 121
Terrasses,
    St-Valery-en-Caux, 152
Téteghem, 40
Tilques, 68
Tonnelier, Bergues, 28
Touquet, Le, 72–74
Tour du Roy, Vervins-en-
    Thiérache, 103
Truite d'Argent, Brussels,
    169

Univers, Amiens, 85
Univers, Arras, 23

Val de l'Oise, Etreaupont-en-
    Thiérache, 95
Verger Pilote, Maroilles, 58
Vert Galant, Amiens, 87
Vervins-en-Thiérache, 103
Vierpot, Boeschepe, 29
Vieux Puits, Bony, 88
Vigneron, Reims, 120
Viking, Fécamp, 139
Vinay, 123

Wast, Le, 74
Watou, 184
Wierre-Effroy, 75
Wimereux, 76
Windsor, Calais, 35
Wisques, 70
Wissant, 77

COMMENT FORM

Please complete this form and let us know what you thought of the establishments you visited, irrespective of whether they appear in this guide. All the information that you send us will be used by Le Shuttle Guides to ensure that only the best places are recommended in future editions. Please photocopy this form if you want to comment on more than one establishment.

Name of establishment ....

Address ....

....

....

.... Post code ....

Telephone and/or fax number ....

Type of establishment

Hotel .... ☐   Restaurant .... ☐

Ferme auberge .... ☐   Chambre d'hôte .... ☐

Food or drink shop or outlet .... ☐

Date and duration of visit (if relevant) ....

Comment on existing entry .... ☐   New recommendation .... ☐

Comments (please describe whatever you think is relevant: food, drink, accommodation, service, personal welcome, noise, cleanliness, quality of produce/products, price, price/quality ratio). Please continue on a separate piece of paper if necessary.

....

....

....

....

....

....

....

....

....
....
....
....
....
....
....
....
....
....
....
....
....
....
....
....
....

Your name and address

Mr/Mrs/Miss/Ms/other .... Initials ....
Surname ....
Address ....
....
....
.... Post code ....

Please return your form to:

The Editor, Le Shuttle Travel Guides, Le Shuttle, FREEPOST RCC 2603,
Crawley, West Sussex, RH10 2ZA

No stamp is required if you post the letter in the UK. If you are mailing from
abroad, please add stamps at the appropriate rate.

We might like to publish your name and comments if you recommend a new
entry or support an existing one.
Please tick this box if you do not want your name to be used. .... ☐

As a matter of courtesy and business practice, Eurotunnel would like to keep you
informed about the services and offers the company and its marketing partners
may provide in the future.
If you would prefer not to receive this information, please tick this box. ..... ☐

COMMENT FORM

Please complete this form and let us know what you thought of the establishments you visited, irrespective of whether they appear in this guide. All the information that you send us will be used by Le Shuttle Guides to ensure that only the best places are recommended in future editions. Please photocopy this form if you want to comment on more than one establishment.

Name of establishment ....

Address ....

....

....

.... Post code ....

Telephone and/or fax number ....

Type of establishment

Hotel .... ☐   Restaurant .... ☐

Ferme auberge .... ☐   Chambre d'hôte .... ☐

Food or drink shop or outlet .... ☐

Date and duration of visit (if relevant) ....

Comment on existing entry .... ☐   New recommendation .... ☐

Comments (please describe whatever you think is relevant: food, drink, accommodation, service, personal welcome, noise, cleanliness, quality of produce/products, price, price/quality ratio). Please continue on a separate piece of paper if necessary.

....

....

....

....

....

....

....

....

....
....
....
....
....
....
....
....
....
....
....
....
....
....
....
....
....

Your name and address

Mr/Mrs/Miss/Ms/other .... Initials ....
Surname ....
Address ....
....
....
.... Post code ....

Please return your form to:

The Editor, Le Shuttle Travel Guides, Le Shuttle, FREEPOST RCC 2603,
Crawley, West Sussex, RH10 2ZA

No stamp is required if you post the letter in the UK. If you are mailing from
abroad, please add stamps at the appropriate rate.

We might like to publish your name and comments if you recommend a new
entry or support an existing one.
Please tick this box if you do not want your name to be used. .... ☐

As a matter of courtesy and business practice, Eurotunnel would like to keep you
informed about the services and offers the company and its marketing partners
may provide in the future.
If you would prefer not to receive this information, please tick this box. ..... ☐